same limp shortsightedness which left the victors incapable of establishing a lasting peace after that war.

Turning to an analysis of power itself, Dr. MacIver proves that it has been undergoing a long process of transformation. From the dawn of civilization, when primitive men banded together to form a community of strength, to the rise of modern democracies and the dissolution of empires, he shows how the pattern favoring the broadening of the basis of government has evolved.

Dr. MacIver indicates that true freedom for all mankind depends upon a judicious use of the great power sources—the knowledge, the technological potential, and the wealth of the world. He holds that the pressing problems—the threat of war and relief for the poverty-bound peoples of the earth—can be resolved by immediate utilization of man's emerging resources with a modicum of intelligence. And he sets forth the changes that must be made now—with armed peace far too precarious to be accepted with complacency.

In addition to his long career as an educator, Dr. MacIver has written many books, among them THE MODERN STATE, SOCIETY, DEMOCRACY AND THE ECONOMIC CHALLENGE, and THE WEB OF GOVERNMENT. He served on government committees during and after the war. He is currently President of the New School for Social Research.

POWER
TRANSFORMED

POWER
TRANSFORMED

The Age-Slow Deliverance of the Folk
and now the Potential Deliverance
of the Nations from the Rule of Force

R. M. MacIver

THE MACMILLAN COMPANY, NEW YORK
COLLIER-MACMILLAN LIMITED, LONDON

First Printing

THE MACMILLAN COMPANY, NEW YORK
COLLIER-MACMILLAN CANADA, LTD., TORONTO, ONTARIO

Library of Congress catalog card number: 64-12172

Printed in the United States of America

Contents

POWER
TRANSFORMED

THE MISCALCULATIONS
OF THE MIGHTY
A Historical Exhibit

NOTE FOR PART ONE

This book falls into two quite distinct parts. Part One is written in a more personal vein, being the reflections and conclusions of the writer as he looks back to the peaceful years when men comfortably believed in progress and the triumph of democracy, and as he follows the train of disruption and dissolution, of wasted courage and ravaged lives and the unceasing smell of death, while over an unbelievable world war presided the miscalculating men of power. The crowning miscalculations came with the making of the peace, the slow ripening harvest of which was the greater convulsion of another world war. We cannot turn the page of history in advance, but the half-century that is now exposed to our eyes tells a most revealing tale concerning the miscarriages of power. To point up this tale is the purpose of Part One, since it offers a prime exhibit for the subject treated in Part Two. In this first part the author has felt free to express his conclusions on certain controversial questions on which the verdict of history—if there is such a verdict—is not yet by any means rendered.

1.

The Ending of an
Age of Peace

Having lived through the last generation of a great age of peace—great by any standard of comparison—and through two generations of an age of great wars, I have been increasingly impressed by the manner in which power and folly often go hand in hand.

No one who has grown up in the twentieth century knows what it means to enjoy the sense of peace on earth, to have the assurance that the sun of peace will rise tomorrow as certainly as it has risen today, to plan for the future without fear that some dark news will render the planning vain. Growing up in such an age, the writer feels that he has left not only his youth far, far behind, but also the very world in which he lived. Its lineaments, its geography, its beliefs, its assumptions, its hopes are all consigned to the forever buried past.

The countries that were then the leading powers are no longer in the van. Some powers of importance then have ceased to exist, others have been dismembered or bereft of territories. Of the two emergent world powers one, the United States, had scarcely thought of itself as an international power at all; the other was half-asleep in anachronistic feudalism. Asia and Africa have ceased to be expanses of Western exploitation, carved up or dominated by the regnant West. In Asia a vast new Communist power has assumed a formidable position, while the India that was then "the brightest jewel in the British Crown" has become an independent republic. In tropical Africa, then wholly colonialized except for Ethiopia and the little republic of Liberia, an ever-increasing number of new republics have emerged out of tribalisms on a surge of still unachieved nationalism.

Not only has the map of the earth been transformed, but also the minds of its inhabitants everywhere—their attitudes, their beliefs, their expectations, their credulities and fears. There is always a new age waiting to be born, but this new age did not come as the slow birth of time but was midwifed by violence and disaster. As philosophers have said often enough, good and evil often spring from the same stem. Out of evil good may come, and out of good, evil, according to the degree of wisdom men learn in evil times or forget in good ones. Folly is never justified of its children, but the evil it produces may, at a heavy price, be in some measure redeemed by later wisdom.

So it came about that a new age was born before its appointed season, though with unprecedented travail that did not end at the birth. Changes that had been slowly breaking through the surface exploded into full being. Ideas that had striven to win acceptance against all the odds were catapulted into great action systems. The mighty were pulled down from their seats and peasants became the masters of empires. Whole divisions of mankind that had been branded with inferiority broke the links that bound them to the traditions of the past. Many changes that had been slowly advancing were swept forward on the surge of the violent eruptions of the new times. But they all bore the insignia of the violence in which they had arisen.

It is hard to think back to the more tranquil age when social and political change was neither drastic nor associated with violence—the age of my youth. My early lot was cast in a remote island off the west coast of Scotland while Victoria was still the great and glorious queen in the eyes of the people. Great Britain was the metropolitan of a world-encircling empire and the mistress of the seas. She was the guardian of the peace, the balancer of power over the whole earth. Her long period of peace had been a time of steady growth. She was the leader in industry and in trade, in banking and finance and shipping. The Communists, being perhaps more adept in wishful thinking than other men, have denounced capitalism as the great and only warmaker. On the contrary, the record shows that capitalism abhors the disruption and destructiveness of great wars, and did so even before it learned that great wars are themselves progenitors of Communism. We might further observe that the capitalism Communists purport to describe has a mythical element in it, since the reality has itself undergone a century-long process of change into socio-capitalism.

In that deep-buried age of my youth news traveled more slowly, but then we had rarely any anxiety about what the news might contain. There was no radio, and television was unconceived. On my native island we even had no telephones until I was well in my teens. No airplane had as yet cast its swift shadow over the earth. So in Britain we could still bless the narrow sea that kept us apart and the more secure. The world seemed to us to revolve around Great Britain. We were beyond the range of European troubles. Europe, we thought, was motley, beset by uneasy divisions and ancient enmities. Britain, with her democracy that still respected persons according to their place in the scheme of things, with her great factories and her bustling ports, was the acme of civilization. The benefits therefrom had flowed out over Western Europe and would in due time spread across the world. We had occasional difficulties with the French and with the Germans, and there were two opposing alliances to which they respectively belonged, but when we put our weight on one side against the other, our superior power and our diplomacy would maintain the balance of peace. The French were behind us in industry and trade. They had style and politesse but were sadly deficient in morals. As for the Germans, they were catching up and they certainly had to be watched. They were ingenious and efficient and pushing, and Prussia still smacked of the barbaric militarism of bygone days. Beyond these two countries there were mostly minor peoples of no particular consequence to the scheme of things. Austria-Hungary was not a country but a patched-together congeries of centrifugal ethnic groupings.

There was of course Czarist Russia, a sprawling backwardness of mujiks and Cossacks ruled over by a ruthless but inefficient aristocracy. And across the Atlantic there was the land of our own kin, a half-developed continental expanse where they grew bountiful harvests of wheat and maize and tobacco and cotton. Alas, through some obstinate bungling under a bad-tempered king, they had defected from the great motherland. They were concerned with their own affairs, exploiting their own big land, and lived apart from the great movements of the age. We had no quarrel with them, and they served a very useful purpose, because the disgruntled and the dispossessed migrated there in great numbers, for the benefit of all concerned.

In this world of progress we regarded great wars as belonging to the barbaric past. We had no conscription. We saw soldiers rarely, mainly in colorful parades on national occasions, pennants flying, bands playing when it wasn't the skirling of the bagpipes. We could travel at will to foreign countries, without passports or visas. Spies belonged to romantic fiction, with Scarlet Pimpernels and the Three Musketeers. In school we went in heavily for patriotism—but we did not go in for ritual salutes to the flag or oath recitations. It was all by way of laudation of the great empire, flaunting its red stretches across the great map of the world on the schoolroom wall, and the heroic past that created it. We read heart-stirring ballads about "Nelson and the North" and the episode of the "Little Revenge" and the "Burial of Sir John Moore." We sang rousing ditties about "Hearts of Oak" and the "Mariners of England" and Britannia ruling the waves. History was mainly the epic of how the long British struggle for freedom culminated in our unique system of parliamentary democracy and of how in the course of it the brave little island, under Providence, repulsed the enemies that threatened it, grew great and imperial, and became the warrior Keeper of the Peace over all the earth.

The nineteenth century was the greatest of all the centuries, the fruition of the long making of mankind, and the twentieth would soon become its happy heir. There were, it was true, large dark portions of the earth, inhabited, as our poet of empire put it, by "lesser breeds without the law." But we were gradually bringing to them too the gifts of civilization, with our missionaries and our traders preparing the way.

Such was the perspective of the land and of the times in which my youth was cast. It was the product of an unprecedented period of economic advancement, of scientific progress, of social welfare legislation, of increasing productivity of labor, and of the world dominance of a great and decently regulated empire. The moralistic complacency of the Victorian Age was lessening but still retained considerable vogue. If its outlook was smugly inconsistent with the deplorable conditions of many factory cities and with much else that went on beneath the respectable surface of social and economic life, it was nevertheless sustained by many decades of a rising standard of living.

These peaceful decades brought to birth the great seminal ideas and discoveries that the twentieth century has in so many unexpected ways exploited, the evocative, revolutionary, and so often double-edged ideas of Faraday and Curie, of Darwin and Mendel, of Lister and Pasteur, of Marx, of Freud, and of many other notable thinkers. The nineteenth century supplied the twentieth with the resources needed for major new enterprises, for the exploration of the hidden nature of man, for the harnessing of the invincible power of the atom, for new achievements in the conquest of disease, for the application of electronics in industry and in other areas, for all the major upheavals in the affairs of men and of nations that the twentieth century in its wisdom and in its major folly has experienced.

These newborn powers man had acquired, as is the way of power, were neutrally available for constructive or for destructive ends. The peaceful spirit of the nineteenth century remained still with us while Planck and Rutherford and Einstein in their convergent theories upturned the established doctrines of cosmic laws and opened up vistas undreamed of by man before, vistas at once grand and awesome. All these amazing advances the twentieth century took, but under conditions that made the gift of power more deadly than it was beneficent. What the scientists and thinkers and industrial engineers achieved, the alien minds of fumbling powerholders devoted to purposes of destruction and in the process sowed the dragon's seeds from which sprang a crop of more vicious and even more calamitous powerseekers.

In my peace-nurtured youth, no visionary prophet foreboded the coming of a time of world wars. Occasionally a poet or a novelist would picturesquely imagine what a great war would be like. There was, for example, Tennyson in "Locksley Hall":

When I dipt into the future far as human eye could see;
Saw the vision of the world, and all the wonder that would be. . . .
Heard the heavens fill with shouting, and there rain'd a ghastly dew
From the nations' airy navies grappling in the central blue.

But no bombs fell from these airy navies, and the poet went on comfortably in the true Victorian faith:

Yet I doubt not thro' the ages one increasing purpose runs,
And the thoughts of men are widen'd with the process of the suns.

Once in my own boyhood a picture of potential war doom flashed into my mind. A mile out of town there was a battery installation where the naval reservists—of whom our island had many, drawn from the fishing population—used on occasion to get shooting practice. One morning I heard the booming of the guns, a sound to which we usually paid little attention. The day before, a naval flotilla had visited the harbor, including one of the proud new "dreadnoughts." On the late evening of that summer day when the guns were heard, a red sunset spread far across the western sky. Watching it I suddenly imagined it was the glow of burning cities in the land that lay far across the water, glowing in the death silence when the work of the guns had ceased. It made a deep impression on me, one that recurred in later years when the picture became true. But the thought was utterly remote from the orderly balance of the time.

The years of the long peace were moving on to their unenvisioned end while the writer, having a bent for learning, spent a more or less cloistered life as a student at two great universities and then as a lecturer at a third, where in due course he settled down as a happily married man, a householder, and a parent. During these years his academic interest had changed from the subjects in which, following the tradition of the times, he had been educated, the classics, philosophy, ancient history, with a tincture of mathematics, to the then little-reputed social sciences and to the least regarded of them all, sociology. The circumstances of his upbringing had led him to become a somewhat critical observer of the social arena. This attitude began as a revolt against the puritanic pressures of the theological dogmas that prevailed in his home environment, which led in turn to wider questionings.

I was particularly responsive to the utterances of Milton and J. S. Mill and of poets like Blake concerning the freedom of the mind, agreeing that it was the first and greatest of all freedoms, and the most necessary for the welfare of society. I wanted to be a student of society more than of anything else. It is this interest that has prompted all my writings, not least the present one.

In the last years of peace my critical outlook led me into academic trouble, thanks to the gentleman in whose department I was a lecturer. He was deeply offended because I wrote an article in which I raised a number of objections to the political theory of the German philosopher Hegel. My professor-boss was a follower of his, and he took my article as an attack on himself, which was certainly not my intention. So deeply was he offended that he cut off all personal relations with me. Since I had no tenure, and certainly no testimonial from him, I was in urgent need of a new position and was fortunate enough to get an invitation to a Canadian institution, the University of Toronto.

Meanwhile the storm clouds began to loom up over Europe. An Austrian archduke was assassinated by a Bosnian revolutionist, no doubt a shocking event but by no means epoch-making, for assassinations were not so rare in turbulent southeast Europe. This archduke, however, was heir to the throne of the Austro-Hungarian Empire, and the event happened at a time when there were troubles and armed outbreaks in the Balkans. The assassin was a Serbian citizen, and Austria-Hungary and Serbia had been at feud since some years earlier when Austria-Hungary had annexed Bosnia and Herzegovina. This same exhibition of imperialism had caused tension between Russia and Austria-Hungary. It was one of those messy situations that were by no means unfamiliar to that portion of Europe. Austria insisted on strong repressive measures in Serbia and found the Serbian response unsatisfactory. Russia insisted that Serbia must not be attacked by Austria. Serbia mobilized, Austria mobilized and declared war on Serbia. Russia mobilized.

It was a time when high statesmanship was needed, and it was tragically lacking. Negotiations still went on between the great powers, for they were all concerned. France was allied with Russia, Britain had an "agreement" with France, Germany was allied with Austria-Hungary. The negotiations were crossed with misunderstandings and suspicions. The British prime minister, Sir Edward Grey, sought to intervene, proposing a conference, but without the forcefulness or the declaration of Britain's stand that the occasion called for. None of the powers wanted a major war, but when the statesmen falter the militarists win out. So the First World War began.

It was an amazing and horrifying revelation of how the entanglements, the "national interests," and the shortsighted policies of rulers and statesmen could thrust a continent, and finally a large portion of the world, into the furnace of war. It was the greatest exhibit ever offered of the true form of tragedy, the situation in which the failings of high-placed men, and not their villainies, occasion great disasters. In human affairs there is often a fatal disproportion between the ends men seek and the consequences of their seeking. To discipline guilty little Serbia, Austria triggered a series of actions and counteractions revealing at every step the incapacity of the men of power to control the momentum of the process, bringing about at the last the annihilation of all the objectives of all concerned.

Sometimes the propaganda-fed peoples are at least as responsible for a war as are their leaders. It was so in the Spanish-American War. Sometimes the expansionist designs or the brutal encroachments of one country over another have made it necessary that leaders and people meet the forces of aggression with the forces of resistance. Most often, it has been rulers alone who in their clashing ambitions have brought the calamities of warfare upon their people. But there was no deliberate foreplanning of this war, only the debacle of statesmanship, wherein leaders failed to break through the entanglements of their commitments and their power concerns. On the one side strategy was blinded by the pride of position and power—so it was with Russia and Austria—on the other it was paralyzed by lack of timely resolution—so it was with Britain and in degree with France. Because of these shortcomings, the physically fit youth of many lands were drawn into the death pits of the trenches, where millions on millions were mutilated or killed, and great territories were scorched and ravaged, and millions on millions of wives and mothers and sweethearts passed through the long agony of waiting for loved ones so many of whom returned no more. And, during it all, hatred and cruelty and falsehood and the devaluation of human life thrust back the levels that civilization had attained. Great sacrifice, great pain, the gross consumption of human valor may be redeemed by the high goals for which they were given, but when the end of it all is net loss and a more grievous disorder, the damning exposure of the mismanagement of power is complete.

I happened to be in London when war was declared. The attitude of the people was generally one of hushed and somber benumbment. In the days immediately prior to the British declaration of war, I watched crowds of aliens queueing up outside the offices where they received instructions for their departure, mostly younger men obligated to military service. I particularly observed one longish line of German nationals. There was no sign of animation. In stolid silence they responded to the call, like men who feel themselves the playthings of a fate they could do nothing about. There may have been revolutionary fervor in Belgrade. In Berlin the sight of marching troops may have aroused the huzzahs of some street crowds. But if ever there was a war that the peoples did not want or make, it was this war.

After war broke out, the governments concerned issued their respective statements justifying their actions, explaining their endeavors to achieve a peaceful settlement and casting the blame on the obduracy and the devious machinations of the other side in the dispute. In company with a historian colleague I studied these manifestoes, "white papers" and "blue papers," and other-colored documents. The statements seemed to us inconclusive and at some points internally inconsistent, and there were hints at secret agreements that the records did not reveal. What alone was clear were the misconceptions, suspicions, ambitions, and high-handed jealousies that bedeviled the immediate issue and contributed to the catastrophe.

I could see in such a war nothing but evil for all the countries involved. I was greatly concerned over the policy of my own country, feeling it could have done much more to prevent the war had it acted more promptly and more decisively. Before the die was cast I wrote a letter to the London *Times*—but never published—asserting the strong mediating role Britain with its balancing power could play. It seemed as though the governments of Europe were so deeply entangled in their historical feuds and dynastic traditions and diplomatic formulas that they had neither the will nor the vision to avert the impending doom.

2.

The World at War
and the Evil Peace

In normal times so great a change of scene as comes with migration to a new continent might be expected to give one an uplift of novelty and fresh experience. But the shadow of the world war lay over everything, though not so heavily over my new land as over the one I had left. It dulled my response to my new prospects, since I regarded this war as an irremediable blow to all the values of our civilization, and my imagination, unhardened to the wholesale wastage of youth in war, was obsessed by the thought of the constant stupid slaughter it involved. Canada too was at war, for the rule was still accepted that when Britain was at war, Canada was also. What part it would play in the war remained its own affair. A Canadian expeditionary force, fed by young men from the prairies and the maritimes and the central provinces and British Columbia, was being prepared to go overseas and many of them to perish for a cause

15

wholly remote from their ken. I remember thinking, in the style of a Shakespearean reflection: What's Serbia to them or they to Serbia?

One thing that interested me was the impact of the war on Canada. To the great majority of her people, Europe, even Britain, was quite remote. They had a different way of life as well as a different sky, and their major concern as a people was entirely their own. It was the development of a vast terrain populated very thinly along the southern belt of a continental stretch that remained largely unexplored. Particularly in the earlier part of the war, ordinary folk went about their daily concerns as though the country was still at peace. On the whole, except in Quebec, an enclave that tended to live within itself, sentiment was definitely in favor of Great Britain and her allies, though there were groups who disliked to see Canada committed to a state of war.

The war itself went its grim way, with nothing of encouragement for the allies. Its area was expanding, Japan having joined the allies with Italy following at a later date, while Turkey and, later, Bulgaria joined the Central Powers. It was a vortex that drew country after country into it. The Germans, concentrating their forces in the West, took the French by surprise through a flanking movement into and through Belgium, thence sweeping into northern France. Then the impetus of invasion was halted, and there ensued the deadliest stalemate in the history of warfare, along the respective trenches of the opposing fronts. For three years the guns thundered across the no-man's-land between the lines of trenches, and there were furious attacks "over the top," and still the dreary bulletins told of "no change on the Western front." No change—except for the millions who suffered in the stinking trenches, dreading the mutilation or death that came to so many of them, while their leaders knew no tactics except to stage vain slaughterous raids across the top. While the war of attrition went on in the West, the Germans were advancing in Russia; the Balkans were ravaged in bitter fighting; the Turks were engaged with the Russians; the British had some difficult successes in Mesopotamia followed by counteroffensives by the Turks and the Russians; the British, French, and Japanese seized German colonial territories; and on the seas there were battles and great destruction of shipping. An intelligent being looking down on the earth during these years would have concluded that an epidemic of madness had overtaken the race that named itself sapiens, the knowing one.

By the end of 1916 both sides had suffered enormous losses, and there was widespread feeling of exhaustion and futility. It was then that what seems to this writer a calamitous blunder was made by the statesmen of the Allies. Early in 1916 President Wilson conceived that an occasion might well arise when both sides would be ready to accept a mediated peace, and, after his reelection as President in November of that year, he believed the time was ripe. The Germans had already made some overtures, but, coming from a position of strength and being somewhat vague, they were regarded by the Allies as a strategic move rather than a genuine offer and were accordingly rebuffed. President Wilson immediately followed by making his own approach to the belligerents, asking them severally to state the terms on which they would be willing to make peace, combined with guarantees to assure the stability of the peace. The Germans and their allies replied responsively, suggesting a conference to sound out possible terms as a basis for peace. The Allies laid down their terms, but, under the conditions then existing, they were obviously ones the enemy would not accept. They included, for example, reparations and the expulsion of the Turks from their European territories. The Germans at a later date communicated to Wilson their own terms. They were less intransigent, though they included the return to Germany of the portion of Alsace they occupied.

The formidable demands of the Allies ended the prospect opened by the peace overtures. The Germans in turn, very unwisely as it turned out, decided to risk American intervention and resort to all-out submarine warfare, since they believed that in this way they could rather speedily win a decisive victory over Britain. Not long thereafter, when American ships began to be torpedoed, the United States declared war.

It is far from a certainty that, had the British reply to Wilson been less uncompromising, peace might have been concluded two years before it came. There were obstacles in the way, perhaps the most serious being the French insistence on the return to them of Alsace, which was mainly German-speaking and had been ceded along with Lorraine to the Germans after the Franco-German War. Reasonable modes of settlement, particularly an agreement on a plebiscite of the people of Alsace, might have been rejected. This formula was adopted by the French after the defeat of Germany in 1918, but then the French were already in undisputed control. Another big problem was created by the fact that the Germans were still occupying extensive Allied territory both in the East and in the West. The Allies, it is true, had taken over the German colonies but had little else in the way of positive successes. Nevertheless there were considerations that could have made possible a reasonable peace through continued negotiations, if only they had been allowed to start. The agreement to negotiate would have itself opened a prospect to the war-torn peoples that would have evoked a strong drive for a settlement. The stalemate on the Western front, the more decisive area, was exceedingly costly. In order to break it, the Germans had launched a terrific assault at a key point, Verdun, and after many months of incessant fighting had been driven back to where they started—and nearly three-quarters of a million troops had perished there. The battle of the Somme had been even more deadly, where after three and a half months the Allies won a few insignificant miles —and the cost to the British, French, and Germans was altogether around a million men. To this hideous slaughter and mutilation there seemed no end. Were it not that war dulls the sense of humanity, this consideration alone would have impelled the statesmen on both sides to have explored every avenue along which a decent peace might be reached.

Moreover, the Allies had a valuable bargaining point at this time. The United States had shown itself considerably more favorable to the Allied side, and in its Eastern sector there was some sentiment for intervention on that side. Had the Allies accepted and the Germans rejected the peace proposals along the lines put forward by Wilson, this sentiment would undoubtedly have been greatly strengthened, and the Germans certainly were anxious to prevent the accession to the Allies of what might very well be, and proved in the end to be, the decisive factor against them.

Finally, there was the evidence, disregarded by the wishful thinking of the Allies, that by the end of 1916 the Russian people were becoming disaffected and their troops demoralized. The Russian armies had taken the offensive and had won considerable victories, but they were grossly impeded by governmental inefficiency, which among other failures had been responsible for quite inadequate transportation, and their offensive had been halted with heavy losses. The mounting discontent jeopardized their entire war effort. Had the prospect of a not too distant peace been opened up, it might have reinforced their morale and prevented the fateful developments that followed.

We have been contemplating might-have-beens, always a precarious resort. But was there ever a might-have-been more crucial than this one? Was there ever a choice between alternatives that made so momentous a difference to mankind? Had there been more foresight, more rational weighing of the alternatives, had the leaders put the considerations of human welfare above considerations of prestige and possession and the pride and power of victory, there would have been no Hitler, no Mussolini, and in all likelihood no Lenin. In the first place the nations would have been spared two more years of suffering and slaughter, and the peace attained would not have been the vengeful peace of victorious powers. Five million Jews would have been saved from a horrible death in the annihilation camps of the Nazis. Russia would have undergone a very different revolution without the extremity of Bolshevism. Some inevitable changes, such as the industrialization of Russia and the East and the rise of many new independent ex-colonial states would have advanced more slowly, but the world would not today have been divided into two hostile camps armed to the teeth against one another, after the ravage of the Second World War that ended in the mushroom clouds over Hiroshima and Nagasaki.

Democracies are generally the friends of peace, but they would seem to be bad peacemakers. Since war is hated by the majority of the people, they must cherish a blazing sense of the wickedness of the enemy who is causing them so much suffering and loss. So war arouses in them the urge for vengeance, for retribution at any cost, and this spirit grows in vehemence in the face of shattered lives and homes, of the mutilations and the atrocities that are never absent from warfare. Unlike the more military-minded peoples who still think—or thought—of war as an instrument of national policy and therefore calculate, to some degree, the conditions of peace that would achieve it, democracies must regard a war in which they are engaged as a struggle between God and the devil. It becomes necessary to wipe out the devil, to destroy his power to rise again. As a compensation for all the sacrifices of war, they expect the peace to usher in a glorious liberation for mankind. So the war becomes a war to end all wars, to make the world safe for democracy, to create an indissoluble union of all the "peace-loving nations under the reign of law."

If in the midst of the First World War the democratic Allies were intransigent over peace terms, they proved even more so in the midst of the Second, when the Casablanca Conference proclaimed their insistence on "unconditional surrender." It is significant that this demand came from the heads of the two major democracies involved, and was for strategic reasons not supported by the man of power who ruled over the other great ally, the Russian dictatorship.

The wartime spirit animated the last and worst of the blunders of the statesmanship of the First World War, the actual peace terms decided on by the allies. Clemenceau, the "tiger," cried out for the spoliation of the prostrate enemy. He demanded the Saar Valley and the left bank of the Rhine and much else besides. And Lloyd George was all for heavy punishment, while his friends called for the hanging of the Kaiser. Lloyd George, it must be said, knew better, realizing the future peril of excessive and prolonged reparation, but he was the politician catering to the feelings of the crowd. No one reflected back to the origins of the war, which was not caused by the German deviltry, the "Hun" barbarism, to which it was now attributed, but by the miscalculations and the incapacities of a group of rulers and statesmen who allowed an international problem to get out of hand. Wilson alone among the leaders showed any real forethought, opposing the more extreme demands of France and England. Nevertheless the Treaty of Versailles imposed on Germany, in addition to various material exactions and the loss of terrain and of her colonies, a colossal debt extending over a period of thirty years. It is hardly necessary to say that the debt was never paid up, but the treaty remained in force long enough to arouse deep resentment among the rising generation and to fan the chauvinisms that smoldered in the German people. So at the fateful hour they were prepared to follow the frenetic leader who emerged from obscurity to lead them into the abyss. The peace that was to end all wars was such as to breed an even more monstrous war.

The miscalculations of power are a commonplace of history, and I have sometimes pondered how it could be that men of high standing and much experience are so often beguiled into such miscalculation. It is of course obvious that when men are under the influence of strong emotions their judgment is likely enough to be skewed; they are less inclined to weigh the consequences of the actions to which their emotions impel them. But the possessor of power miscalculates not so much because of the strength of his emotion but because power tends to make men feel aloof from and superior to their fellows. They give commands and other men obey. And this habit of command leads them often enough to regard their decisions as intrinsically superior. What they will is right, and hence they do not seriously consider what the reactions will be of those who feel the weight of their power. Thus they miscalculate, their judgment is blinded by the pride of power. But this is a subject to which we must later return.

In the year following the Treaty of Versailles the famous economist, John Maynard Keynes, published *The Economic Conse-*

quences of the Peace. In it he wisely predicted some of the evils
that treaty would create, but no one could then have foreseen the
full train of consequences, or the way in which certain economic
consequences would conspire with political consequences to produce at length a vast world tragedy the consequences of which
still plague the earth, the endless progeny of trouble begotten by
the major folly of the peace.

When in the Hall of Mirrors the Allied chiefs put their sig-
natures to that treaty, did they pause to consider what in the
years ahead the growing generation of a then prostrate power
would think and do about the continuing burden and humiliation imposed upon them? Did they perhaps blandly imagine that
the "punishment" would teach them never to make war again?
They did considerable thinking about the territories they would
respectively annex and the war costs they would recoup. So in
the false name of retributive justice, they gratified the passion for
revenge on enemies who, no less than their own peoples, had undergone an extremity of suffering.

Before it came to the evil peace, in the last stages of the war,
the lack of Allied wisdom was exhibited in other ways. The Allies had naturally been concerned to keep the tottering Russians in
the war, but the steps they took were ill-conceived. The tide of
insurgence was running too high for minor aid and minor intervention. When the Menshevik Revolution took place, Kerensky
made the vain attempt to revive some offensive operations in a
situation where his own position was precarious. The upshot was
the Bolshevik Revolution which ended all that, and there followed the peace treaty of Brest-Litovsk. Lenin signed it tongue in
cheek. The Bolsheviks never intended to comply with its terms,
biding their time. The Communists on seizing power made a general proclamation for an immediate armistice between all the bel-

ligerents and the start of negotiations for a peace "without annexations or indemnities." It was more in the nature of a revolutionary broadcast than a specific approach to the warring governments and was ignored. But the Germans in negotiations with Russia did agree to "no annexations and no indemnities," provided the Allies forthwith accepted the same principle—and the Allies did not. Nor had they done it earlier in the same year when the Pope had made peace proposals, including the same stipulations. At no time did the Allies state their peace terms for purposes of negotiation, one main reason being the secret agreements they had made respecting their several territorial aims. Yet by the end of 1917 the time had come when multitudes yearned for peace, and one British figure, Lord Lansdowne, made public a moving plea in favor of negotiations without total victory. There was still the horrendous stalemate on the Western front with its memories of Arras and the Aisne and Ypres and Cambrai, and if Russia was out of the war the United States was in, with its vast new strength. But the Allied statesmen, most of them, still had no ears for compromise.

After Brest-Litovsk, the French proposed to their Allies the despatch of military forces into Russia to resurrect the Eastern front. This foolhardy proposal was turned down by the British and the Americans. Nevertheless, sometime later, the Allies, and mainly the British and the Americans, committed themselves to military action within Russia, first against the German forces below Murmansk and afterward on the side of the "white" generals who were spasmodically resisting the Moscow government. All these expeditions were unfortunate and wasteful. The efforts to support separately warring "white" generals were based on a failure to realize the intensity of the revolt against the old order in Russia, a failure fostered by the strong distaste felt for the Communist regime, but they merely accentuated the hatred the Bolsheviks felt toward the "capitalists."

The passions of wartime generate blunders more dire than those to which men of power are prone in times of peace. In the difficult many-angled business of politics, even the wisest men will slip and miscalculate at times. But the blunders we cite do not belong to the honest failures of men who misread the signs and failed to solve hard and confusing problems. They contained instead an element of weakness and folly, for they involved an unwillingness to examine and to assess the alternatives of action. The evidences that pointed toward a different policy were unconsidered or disregarded. As a scholar, these blunders had for me a melancholy fascination. My major interest lay in the observation and study of human relationships. My reading of history convinced me that the possession of high power tended to make the possessor inconsiderate of the reactions that might ensue from policies that gave him an immediate gratification and thus prone to errors that recoiled on himself. This tendency seemed to be receiving in this period most tragic illustration.

During this period I was in some measure relieved from brooding on such thoughts by the heavy load of work I was carrying. In addition to my university duties I had been made vice-chairman—in effect, acting chairman, because my chief was a senator who had plenty else to do—of the Dominion of Canada War Labor Board. One part of its task was planning for the relocation of soldiers and munitions workers in peacetime employments—when the war was over. There was real satisfaction in having a job that contemplated the return to peace.

The vast relief peace brought, peace of any kind, obscured at first the potential menace of the terms. Moreover, was there not an assurance against the conditions that had bred the war in the establishment of the League of Nations, the first genuine approach to the reign of international law? Accepting the forward-looking plan of Woodrow Wilson, the Allies had set up a forum of the nations, designed to safeguard the peace and refer any threatening dispute to adjudication, arbitration, or inquiry by the Council of the League. The "tiger" of course didn't believe in it and other elder statesmen were sceptical, but the new generation, which had learned so well what war meant to them, would make it work.

That promise faded soon enough. The League was built on shaky foundations. It presumed an established order that it could sustain and that would sustain it. But the character of the peace terms and the rampant nationalisms the war had accentuated in the peoples who found its provisions unfavorable to their aspirations dimmed the promise the League offered. And the League itself received a heavy blow at the outset, when the Senate of the United States mustered enough negative votes to defeat the adherence of the power that had been its major sponsor.

It is significant of the attitudes of postbellum peacemakers that peace treaties have on the average endured intact only for two or three years. The peace treaties of 1919 endured longer, save for some minor concessions. The harvest of the peace took a generation to ripen, but the crop the next generation reaped was more deadly than the worst forebodings could have conceived.

3.

The Spineless Years

The relaxation of spirit that followed the war was in keeping with the magnitude of the strains it had imposed. It was a time when ideals were discounted and aspirations flagged. The physical reconstruction, the restoration of bombed cities and of shattered industrial equipment, was not accompanied by the reestablishment of the prewar semiaccord between the nations or by any dedication to the greater international order envisaged in the establishment of the League of Nations. In this time of disillusionment, the first international organization designed to assure the supremacy of peace was gradually eroded, by jealousies, suspicions, and nationalistic aggressions, into the memorial of a lost cause.

The memory of bygone sufferings is fleeting, and it is of little account in the historical record. The events that caused them may be notable, but the human costs remain an untold story. The sufferings the war brought on mankind were incalculably great, too great to be reckoned or even conceived, but they left no imprint behind. We feel the sufferings of those near and dear to us, and any sudden disaster that has spectacular features strikes at the hearts of men. When the *Titanic* went down with over sixteen hundred lives, the calamity was tragic drama, and it evoked a gasp of horror in many a land. But the sufferings of the millions who perished in the war, on land and on sea, and of the many more millions to whom it brought grave grief, failed to reach home to us. When suffering becomes multitudinous, the mind safeguards itself against so intolerable an exposure.

So the prime lesson the war taught was soon dimmed, and the most meaningful of all monuments that could have been erected in honor of those who fought and those who died received little credence and little enough support. Institutions live by being believed in, and this institution, though it showed some measure of effectiveness at the start, lived on only as an invalid until it passed away in failure.

In Canada, where I lived then, we watched closely the battle for the League that was waged across the border. Wilson was greatly admired in Canada, and never more than during his last days when he spent his failing strength in working and traveling and pleading for his cause. There was an understandable revulsion in the United States against the ruthless scramble for territorial spoils at Versailles and the nationalistic designs that contended at the peace table and after the "settlement." But this revulsion still left a considerable majority in support of the League, and it by no means explains the venomous attacks of its chief enemies, in whom partisan politics conspired with an isolationist hatred for the peoples of Europe. These enemies, led by the vindictive Senator Henry Cabot Lodge, prevailed, and the minority of Senators who went along with him mustered the more than a third negative votes that sufficed to defeat the ratification of the treaty. The battle over the League was renewed in the presidential election of 1920, when, after a campaign that played on every string of prejudice and suspicion, the candidate favoring the League was defeated by the equivocal nonentity, Warren G. Harding.

The peace brought to the world little of the spirit of peace. It was divisive in intention and even more divisive in results. In Eastern Europe the dispossessed and the disgruntled peoples created new troubles. The Poles made military forays over several fronts, against Lithuania and Czechoslovakia and Russia. The Greeks invaded Anatolia, and the Italian freebooter, D'Annunzio, seized Fiume for a spell. The collection of German reparations became increasingly difficult, defaults being followed by threats and ultimata. The French, who throughout this period displayed the most intransigent attitude, regardless of consequences, invaded the Ruhr along with the Belgians, and fomented strife in the Rhineland, eager to separate it from Germany. The German government resorted in desperation to a galloping inflation of the currency, being otherwise faced with total bankruptcy. After the French occupation of the Ruhr, the mark fell so precipitately that it sank at length to a trillionth of a gold mark! It is hard for anyone who was not an eyewitness of the situation to realize the profound effect it had on the spirit of the German people. The government wiped out its public debt, and brought confusion to the French in the Ruhr, but at a terrible price. To the German people it was as though the ground were sinking, sinking beneath their feet. Savings were swept away; no value, no standard, no firmament remained. The big owners, the industrialists and the landlords, made substantial profits. But it was bad for capitalism, it

was bad for the struggling Weimar democracy, it was good for
Communism and very good for the now unbridled so-called National Socialism of Adolf Hitler.

The financial debacle in Germany had adverse repercussions
in other countries also, not least in France, where the franc fell
considerably. Great Britain and the United States became particularly concerned, and the Dawes Plan was put into effect, providing for the reorganization of the Reichsbank, a new basis for
reparations payments, and a loan to Germany of eight hundred
million gold marks. To sustain the payment of reparations, the
creditors were now lending a large sum to the debtor.

The one really hopeful development in this chaotic time was
the Locarno Conference, where the conferees agreed on a series
of arbitration treaties and reciprocal guarantees between the countries of Western Europe, including arbitration pacts by Germany
with Poland and with Czechoslovakia. It looked as though Germany was already being incorporated into a meaningful system
for the assurance of peace. The "spirit of Locarno" was hailed as
the harbinger of a new era. But the flush of hope proved short-
lived. Mutual distrust prevailed over mutual assurance. The powers were putting their reliance on bilateral defensive treaties more
than on the Locarno guarantees. The French, with the pathetic
kind of pesudohindsight that takes measures to prevent the re-
currence of a bygone situation rather than to provide against the
conditions of the new emergent situation, built the Chinese Wall
called the Maginot Line. But of all the unavailing recourses of this
leaderless time none was so grandiosely futile as the much-lauded
Pact of Paris, initiated as the Briand-Kellogg Pact, under which
the nations unanimously pledged themselves to renounce *aggressive* war. What government will ever admit that the war in which
it engages is one of aggression on its part? What invader ever

fails to recount the grievances and wrongs it has suffered on the part of the invaded country? No criteria of aggression were set up in the Pact of Paris, but that is not surprising. Neither the League of Nations nor in its turn the United Nations was able to find a satisfactory formula by way of definition. At best only a tribunal could decide such an issue, and there was no tribunal. Nor did the Pact stipulate any sanctions to be applied against a state that was preparing or carrying out an act of aggression.

In spite of diplomatic blunderings, reparations, war debts, and nationalistic economic policies, a very considerable recovery was advancing in the war-devastated lands. It is a remarkable testimony to the indomitable will of man that he so speedily transformed the rubbled chaos of shattered cities into new factories and residential areas better designed than before. But the passions and the mind wounds of war are not so quickly obliterated as the evidences of material destruction. They still seethed beneath, waiting their time.

The first clear sign of the wave of the future appeared in one of the victorious countries, but it was a disgruntled and ambiguous victor. It was the coming to power of Mussolini. Italy was a poor country taken as a whole, and incompetently governed. It had no notable record in the war, and it was resentful because it had been given so small a cut out of the big territorial pie divided at the conference table. This disgruntlement weakened the hold of the government over the right-wing and center parties, while unemployment and economic discontent gave the Communist Party a strong and threatening position, especially in the industrial north. Communist Russia had set the example of dictatorship. The ex-Communist Benito Mussolini saw his opportunity and by an easy *coup d'état* set up his Fascist dictatorship, a rightist semi-imitation of the leftist model.

As the decade wore on, after Locarno brought new hope and the Young Plan made a more acceptable provision for the reparations payments, a real settlement in Europe appeared in the making. But the direction of affairs needed to fulfill that hope was lacking. The first in a critical series of disastrous events happened in the United States, with the stock-market crash of 1929, ushering in the worst and most prolonged depression in a country that had endured many earlier ones. In the first postwar decade, the United States had experienced a very considerable growth of the national wealth. There were, however, some unsound features in its prosperity. Its economic policies were in some respects shortsighted, particularly the mercantile obsession that lifted its tariffs higher and higher. These policies, detrimental in themselves, were in this period more harmful to the war-torn countries whose trade it diminished than to the United States itself. Then there was the factor that was the immediate cause of the depression, the fevered speculation that raised market values far above reasonable expectations of return. Looking back over this period, one must admit that business interests were even more misguided than the statesmen who catered to them, for it was the pressure of business lobbies that instigated the tariff legislation, while our financial leaders for the most part accepted with complacency the pyramiding of stock values.

The crash and the deepening depression in the United States had most unhappy effects on international trade and indirectly on international relations. Americans tended to think of it as merely their own affair, of small concern to the rest of the world. So little was the international nexus of economic activity understood that the Congress, under the persistent lobbying of various special interests, committed the heinous economic sin of passing the grotesquely timed Smoot-Hawley Tariff Act. In vain did the economists of the country, for once united almost to a man, protest. Other countries, hard-hit by the new restrictions, retaliated by countertariffs, giving a new dimension to the depression that was spreading across the civilized earth.

In Europe the depression was highlighted by the failure of the great Austrian bank, the Credit-Anstalt. Austria had been hit not only by the general restriction of international trade but particularly by the tariff policies of the neighboring states that had previously been joined with it in the Austro-Hungarian Empire, as well as by the refusal of France to permit a customs union between Austria and Germany. The cumulation of economic follies and political blunders set in motion one disaster after another. The Bank of England, the major bulwark of international exchange, was unable to stand the strain and had to abandon the gold standard, creating thereby an almost unprecedented feeling of economic insecurity among the nations.

Worst of all, because of the linkage of economic insecurity and political instability, was the effect on Germany. As early as 1923 German reaction and disaffection had found a curious prophet in the youthful son of an Austrian petty customs official. It was the year when French and Belgian troops took occupation of the Ruhr. Adolf Hitler was a supreme egoist and an extreme nationalist, who wanted to go back six hundred years, to the days when the Teutonic Knights were at the height of their power, who hated democracy, despised the bourgeoisie, and at the same time regarded the Germans, the true Aryans, as the master race upon the earth. As leader of the National Socialist Party, he took a vociferous part in the attempt of General Erich Ludendorff to overthrow the Bavarian government—the "Beer Hall Putsch." Imprisoned on its failure, he wrote the Nazi Bible, the reckless inflammatory *Mein Kampf,* a tirade reeking of falsehood and hatred. Thereafter the Nazi Party made practically no headway, although Hitler continued to fulminate and rallied some more followers, until the depression overtook Germany, which had seemed in the preceding years to have already attained a considerable measure of stability. In 1930 the Nazis became formidable as a political party for the first time. Several of the big German industrialists had come round to Hitler's side with that pathetic readiness to trust, when the boat is rocking badly, the man who promises to bring them safely to port. In 1932 Hitler attained his maximum voting strength, winning 230 seats out of 608. He never won a majority of seats, and in the last election of a year whose turbulence was manifested in a series of rapidly successive elections, his voting power showed a marked decline.

Nevertheless the Weimar Republic was doomed. It may not have been particularly wise or astute in its leadership, but it did carry on with some success under extremely difficult conditions, and it seemed to have weathered the worst of the storm when the new troubles brought on by the depression struck it. Its situation then became most parlous. It was beset by the now strengthened Communist left and by the formidable Nazi right, both ready to gain control by a *coup d'état*. It was Hitler who won out, and without resorting to the violence his party was planning. The ageing President Hindenburg used his authority, when the elections had given no clear verdict and other candidates had proved unable to form a cabinet, to nominate Hitler as his successor.

The world knew, or at least ought to have known, what then to expect. Hitler had made his intentions perfectly clear. He was out to rearm the German people for revenge and for dominion. The Germans were the Herrenvolk, the proper lords of creation. He would lead them to shining triumphs. The Germans had been robbed of victory in the great war by the traitors in their midst, the radicals, the Communists, and above all the Jews. He found in a mysterious brotherhood called "international Jewry" an insidious conspiracy to defeat the master race and to pollute its purity. He would wipe out these criminals and he would destroy the "red terror." So he appealed to that considerable mass which is to be found in every people and which is swelled in times of crisis and disaster, the mass that thinks with its emotions. And to the unemployed he promised new and greater prosperity with full employment. He capitalized on the troubles of the wounded republic by declaiming against the ineptitude and supineness of its government. He pulled out all the stops to play with diabolical skill on the prejudice, the pride, the humiliation, and the deep discontent that seethed in the people. What made him all the more dangerous was that this demagogue meant what he said. He was a demagogue by nature rather than by calculation.

It was a time when high statesmanship was called for, and it was not forthcoming. There were those who thought they could deal with Hitler, there were those who were quietly pleased to see him take power, because he would put the Communists where they belonged. Let us briefly review the situation.

The United States was withdrawn in its isolationism. It had rejected the League, and it had weakened the chances of the World Court by making its adherence depend on a crippling reservation. In face of the growing threat of Hitler and of an alarming rise of Japanese militarism, it passed a series of neutrality acts establishing an embargo on armaments or any resources requisite for war purposes to any belligerent outside of the Americas, no matter how much it might be the victim of aggression. While Hitler was rising to power and for some years thereafter, the United States was almost wholly engrossed with the problems of the great depression. Before it began I had left Canada to take a position at Columbia University, and I had good opportunities to observe how the cumulative disorganization and misery of the depression engrossed the national attention to the almost total exclusion of anything else. This was the more so because the New Deal legislation of the Roosevelt administration excited the fiercest controversy. Believing as I did that strong new measures were necessary, I found it hard to understand the inveterate bitter resentment it evoked from most of the leaders of business and finance, whom it may very well have saved from more grievous troubles. The New Deal was a conglomerate of temporary measures intended to salvage distressed industries and areas and to relieve the plight of agriculture, of permanent economic safeguards of lasting value, and of long-overdue programs of social security. While some of it was hasty and not well-thought-out, on the whole it was one of the few exhibits during these spineless years of resolute constructive action on the part of any democratic government.

The preoccupation with economic problems and with partisan attacks on his program made Roosevelt chary of intervention in the international situation. He feared a rebuff from the Congress, while the isolationist spirit was still strong and controversy still raged over his economic measures. I had a special reason for studying the problems of the time, since the president of Columbia University, Nicholas Murray Butler, had thrust on me the task of assembling a group of leading economists from across the country, along with a few others knowledgeable in public affairs, to work out a policy to combat the depression. Among other things I learned how hard it is for a diversified group of economists to agree on specific proposals.

In Western Europe it was a period of ineffective overtures, partial alliances, and entirely inadequate policies in the face of the ever-increasing menace of Hitler and his gang. No united front was formed to meet it. France and Russia made an alliance for a five-year period, up to 1940. But when in 1938 the surrender at Munich confirmed the doubts of that cold calculator, Stalin, it prepared the way for his fateful deal with Germany. Britain pursued flaccid "understandings" with Hitler and Mussolini. France was in its too common condition of transient makeshift ministries composed of divisive parties beset on the left by the intransigent Communist groups and on the right by equally intransigent reactionaries who were inclined to make terms with Hitler to save themselves from the inroads of Communism.

One can reasonably conjecture that had an inclusive and binding alliance been formed of the countries exposed to the obvious danger of Hitlerian aggression, and had the United States awakened from the false complacency of isolationism and joined the forces of resistance, the Second World War could have been avoided and its endless plague of consequences never been born. Instead, the situation grew more and more out of hand. The swashbuckler of Rome had descended on Ethiopia. The League of Nations summoned up the courage to vote economic sanctions against Italy, but not enough courage to counteract certain economic interests, for they omitted the particular sanction that counted most, an embargo against the sale of oil to Italy. So Mussolini overcame Ethiopia, and soon thereafter the German-Italian Axis was formed. Only the aggressors showed resolution, among them the new-risen General Franco, who with the aid of German and Italian troops destroyed the Spanish republic. The prospects of peace were dimming into darkness.

While the storm clouds thickened in the West, ominous developments were happening in the East, with Japan as the great disturber of the peace. In her war of conquest against Asia, she seized Manchuria, denounced the exceedingly mild report of a League of Nations Commission which would have left her in effective control of that area, but without actual ownership, and forthwith resigned from the League. The ineffectiveness of the League as an instrument of peace was fatally exposed.

Having triumphantly flouted the Versailles Treaty by his rearmament program and by the reoccupation of the Rhineland, Hitler proceeded to annex Austria, with only formal protests from England and France. France was at the time engaged in one of her characteristic attempts to patch together a new government. Britain under Neville Chamberlain kept on asking Hitler for pledges that now he would be good, thus exhibiting a total misunderstanding of the character and the designs of the author of *Mein Kampf*.

Yet the evidence "leaped to the eyes." Who could listen to the broadcasts of the Führer and not recognize the fanaticism and the fury of his mind? And there was evidence enough that he was not only a fanatic but also a scoundrel regardless of honor and of truth. In the year preceding the Austrian *coup* he had resorted to a dastardly stratagem to degrade the high command of the German Army, in order to remove possible resistance to the immediate execution of his military adventures. Field Marshal von Blomberg had married a lady who had been his secretary— an action of itself contrary to the aristocratic tradition of the officer corps. Presently a police dossier appeared that represented the lady as having been a common prostitute. Having thus rid himself of Von Blomberg, Hitler, with the aid of Himmler, confronted the most likely successor, General Werner von Fritsch, with a fake document purporting to show that Von Fritsch was a homosexual who was endeavoring to keep the fact secret by paying blackmail to a convicted criminal. The outraged army corps was able to prove the falsity of the charge, but Hitler paid no heed, dismissed Von Fritsch and made himself the personal commander of the military forces of the Reich. His Blackshirts and his Storm Troopers were now on top, ready to execute without a moment's scruple the will of the master. This was the man whom Chamberlain sought continuously to conciliate. There is an ancient Greek saying that "it is no use singing incantations over a wound that needs the knife."

So Hitler drove ahead and forced Czechoslovakia to yield to his demands. And the ever-hopeful Chamberlain went to Munich and complacently brought back a new "agreement." All that can possibly be said in favor of this hapless surrender is that Britain had failed to make adequate military preparations or to create a united defensive front against the most ruthless aggressor of modern times, a man whose mind was so infected with the poison of racism that he set out to destroy every man, woman, and child of the Jewish people within his borders. If the British and French leaders had hoped that by obtaining a breathing spell they would be in a stronger position to resist Hitler's threats in the future, concentrating on increasing their military power in the meantime, they were the more misguided. Until Munich, Russia was still on the anti-German side in alliance with France, and Italy was certainly unwilling to risk joining up with Hitler, and the Czechs still possessed a by no means negligible army, while in Germany itself a serious military plot to destroy Hitler was in preparation. But Munich changed the whole situation.

Chamberlain was sadly miscast for the role of statesman at this crucial juncture. Perhaps, had he been Prime Minister of Britain in 1914 instead of in 1938, he would have gone down in history as a successful mediator, though no one would ever have known what tragedies for all mankind he had averted. Often enough in the historical record statesmen, anxious to avoid some gross blunder of their predecessors, assume too easily that the situation they face is similar to the older one and make as gross a blunder in acting accordingly. Kaiser Wilhelm was an utterly different type from Führer Hitler and amenable to quite different considerations. The First World War could have been averted by a reasonable amount of diplomatic give-and-take. The Second World War, if it could have been averted at all, could only have been by the marshaling of enough military power to prove even to a Hitler that he could not possibly win. Concessions merely fed his appetite for more, and his power to obtain it. Perhaps in our own day some of our leaders wrongly assume that the situation of 1938 is with us again. But Khrushchev is not Hitler, and it is perfectly obvious to him, as it should be to us, that a nuclear war between great powers could end only in the destruction of them both and of most of the earth besides.

Even before the Nuclear Age, the means of destruction had become formidable enough to make any calculations of the attainment of objectives through major warfare entirely futile. It was so in the First World War, which reduced to vanity and ashes all the policies of all the countries concerned. It was even more so in the Second World War, and if some madness of miscalculation or sheer trigger-pressing accident should launch a third great-power war, the consequences would freeze the blood of those who lived long enough to see them develop. Hitler went to war to be the mighty founder of a millennium of German domination, and some five years later he died a suicide, deserted save for his bride, in an underground bunker in his ravaged capital. And the train of consequences his blind folly evoked still moves incalculably on.

After Munich war was inevitable—unless the insider plot against Hitler succeeded. Fate seemed to be conspiring with the psychopathic of Berchtesgaden. Stalin, eternally distrustful of the good faith of the Allies, saw in the British surrender a sign that England and France would make a deal with Hitler at all costs and then unite with him against Russia. In any event, he would have been not at all loath to see the European "capitalists" ruin one another in a war from which he stood aside, waiting for eventual booty. He had no scruples about abandoning his Western ally. Hitler was thus relieved of his one big fear. He was perfectly willing to negotiate with Russia for a division of the spoils after he had made himself master of Poland and Rumania. When these countries were in his hands, he could proceed to put Stalin in his proper place. For Britain and France he had now come to have nothing but contempt. They were "little worms. I saw them at Munich."

So he prepared to attack Poland. Britain at last stood firm, made preparations for war, and pledged its aid, along with that of France, to the Poles. Last-minute appeals to Hitler, including one from President Roosevelt, were in vain. On September 1, 1939, the German armies crossed the Polish frontier. England and France declared war on Germany. The Second World War began.

I still recall the feel of those last weeks of August, 1939, the sultry tension in which we lived, the clutching to hope against the accumulating evidence of approaching disaster, the surmising whether the United States would somehow be drawn in, the endless listening to the latest radio news, the fear and the anger, the praying and the cursing. I spent these weeks in our quiet summer cottage and had as guest for a few days a distinguished Polish professor of sociology whom, by what proved to be a most happy chance, I had invited over from Poland to participate in the summer program at Columbia University. He was waiting for the departure of the liner on which he was to return. He was

quite unwell and spent most of the day lying blanketed in a
hammock. We implored him to cancel his passage. We even obtained for him a likely position for the fall at a Midwestern university. But no, if the *Pilsudski* went he would go with it. He
had promised the Polish government that if war came he would
carry on some kind of sociological study of the army! So he left
us, but fortunately never reached Poland. German submarines
were lying in wait for the *Pilsudski*, but they mistook for it the
British liner *Athenia* and torpedoed the latter instead, while a
British submarine held up the *Pilsudski* and escorted it to a
Scottish port. That, at least, is the interpretation we put on a
German act that caused Hitler considerable embarrassment, since
it was responsible for the death of twenty-eight American pas-
sengers, and he was most anxious to keep the United States neutral.
It is characteristic of Hitler's reckless disregard for truth that he
had the news published that Churchill gave the order for the sinking of the *Athenia*.

Later on, restored to health in an English hospital, my friend
was able to return to the States where he occupied an important
place in his academic field. It was a happy illustration of the way
in which the play of chance so often decides, for better or for
worse, the destinies of men.

4.

Armageddon

In 1939 the final weapon was still unborn. In 1939, when Hitler launched the new great war, power-greedy rulers could still anticipate the winning of booty and renown out of it. Communist Stalin had made his deal with his new Nazi comrade for the division of Poland. Mussolini was biding his time till he felt it safe to join his ally. The militarists of Japan, linked as they were in a pact with the Axis Powers, rejoiced in the expectation they could now pursue without molestation their aggressions in the Pacific area. The power-greedy masters were all agog, but among the peoples there was no jubilation, no glad ringing of bells.

There seemed to be a fatal madness about this war, initiated by the will of a single fanatic dictator. Here was a people of great achievement, in culture and in industry, suffering the distemper created by a humiliating and burdensome peace, thrust, as it was recovering, into the new misery of a severe depression, and sufficiently befuddled to have allowed its destiny to fall into the hands of a gang of ruthless exploiters. Here were the nations the dictator threatened, so slow in appraising the peril, so distracted by lesser problems, and so divided among themselves, that they permitted this fanatic to go from strength to strength and to bully into submission the weaker neighboring states. And here were the peoples on both sides of the front, all dreading the war that engulfed them all. Surely there was never a more striking exhibit of the follies of power and the misgovernment of men.

This world war had little resemblance to its predecessor, either in its origin or in its development. There was no stalemate punctuated by costly and futile attacks, no endless attrition in the immobility of the trenches. After the ominous stillness of the first winter, it became a war of sweeping advances, with the most deadly onslaughts coming from the skies. In the waiting period of the first winter, the superficial began to speak about the "phony" war. But after the Sitzkrieg came the Blitzkrieg. The Germans first descended on the neutrals Denmark and Norway. Neutrality and the "international law of war" were obsolete conceptions in their eyes. Thereafter Belgium and Holland were crushed, and then came the turn of France. German air power and strategic concentration swept through the French defenses, and in a few weeks French resistance was wholly shattered and an armistice was thereafter signed at Compiègne, where in the First World War the Germans had signed their surrender. By this time Mussolini had found it safe to make his move and stab France in the back, though the stab proved to be little more than a pinprick, demonstrating the weakness of his vaunted power. Perhaps there is more than historical significance in the fact that everyone, without exception, who joined forces with Hitler was thereby consigning himself to perdition.

The Second World War, from beginning to end, was a war that confounded all calculations. To the Allied world the first and

most horrifying of these surprises was the swift debacle of France.
To the United States it came like a jarring electric shock. Until
then the majority of its people had felt no great involvement. Even
though many of them hated Hitler and fervently hoped for the
victory of the Allies, they were glad to be out of it. Now there was
in the air a new grim resolution, an awakening to portended
dangers previously ignored or at most surmised. Isolationism was
finally overcome. The power that had ravished Europe was primarily air power, and against air power the protection of the Atlantic was crumbling. The fear and dislike felt toward the Nazis
was intensifying. Roosevelt, who had hitherto been restrained in
his eagerness to aid the Allies by his politician's sense of what
the Congress would permit, came out emphatically for huge defense expenditures, which were immediately approved, soon to
be followed by billions more.

Overrunning Belgium and northern France, the German armies
had trapped the large British Expeditionary Force, almost en-
circling it so that its line of retreat to the sea was in the gravest
danger. But Hitler failed to close the gap, delaying until it was
too late. By masterly withdrawal strategy the British poured
through the mouth of the trap to the famous evacuation at Dun-
kirk, where an extraordinary flotilla of all manner of seagoing
craft was hastily rushed. Now came, in the romantic words of
the valorous new-risen leader of the British, Britain's "finest
hour." Alone it carried on, harried by squadrons of planes and
tensed for the day when the invading armada would be thrust
against its shores. Good fortune—or providence, as it surely
seemed—was on the side of its fortitude. Hitler, refusing to believe the British would be so mad as not to yield to his invincible
might, delayed "the Sea Lion" operation. His admirals, though
they hardly counted, favored delay for a different reason, be-

lieving that the total blockade of Britain combined with smashing attacks on its nerve centers would be a surer and safer way of reducing Britain to subjection. So the Sea Lion never swam the Channel. The time was postponed again and yet again. Instead, Hitler rained down destruction on army installations, ports, airports, and shipping. The Eagle had taken the place of the Sea Lion.

Fighting against superior odds, the Royal Air Force suffered heavy losses, and the Battle of Britain might have been lost. But another tactical mistake turned the German assault from important military objectives, involving head-on air battles, to tremendous and sustained night bombings of London and other cities, in order to terrify the population into submission. For all the devastation it caused, this strategy nevertheless gave the British the time to build up their air power, and with the aid of their new radar equipment to inflict heavy losses on the invading planes, as well as to roar in destructive might over Germany itself. Britain was saved, and the war went on.

While waiting for Britain to succumb, Hitler now committed his biggest blunder. Power, when intoxicated with success, is peculiarly liable to make disastrous mistakes, always in the direction of excess. The second "little corporal" would outdo the first, the great Napoleon, triumphing where the latter had failed. He would bring Russia to its knees. So was exposed in turn the blunder made by that other man of power, Stalin, when two years earlier he betrayed his ally to make a deal with Hitler. Stalin had been using the opportunity to pick up more spoils than he had bargained for, not only much of Poland but also the three small Baltic states, a chunk of Finland, part of Rumania. Already, before the blow fell, he had become much concerned over the prodigal and unexpected successes of his dangerous "friend," though he still kept showering congratulations on the glorious victor.

If history could teach us, the record of this war would make an invaluable primer. The course of the war defeated all the calculations and nearly all the plans made by all the belligerents. And in particular all the deals, pacts, plots, and counterplots of those who hoped to profit by it boomeranged devastatingly against their authors. There was one pact, however, that breathed a very different spirit, calling for the end of territorial aggrandizement and for the freedom of the peoples. It was the Atlantic Charter, signed on behalf of their respective countries by Franklin D. Roosevelt and Winston Churchill. While it expressed an ideal that is yet a long way from attainment on the earth, the countries that signed it did endeavor, most of the time, to follow it and consequently, so far as they could, they made the peace that ended this war very different from the evil peace of 1919.

We need not trace the events of the war through the slaughterous years that followed. It is enough for our purpose to comment on certain fateful events that belong in history's little-studied lesson book.

The next of the great surprises was the smashing air attack on Pearl Harbor. It was, alas, much more of a surprise than it ought to have been. The United States had some months earlier warned Japan against seeking further military domination in Asia, and the Japanese had countered by bidding the United States not to meddle in Oriental affairs. The Americans had broken the Japanese secret code and had deciphered messages sufficiently indicating Japanese intentions. The British Admiralty had sent Washington a warning of danger from Japan. Hull and Roosevelt were alerted, and they alerted the military chiefs. Why the messages did not register at Pearl Harbor remains somewhat obscure. The only unknown factor was when and where the blow would fall. Two Japanese envoys were in Washington at the time, ostensibly on a peace mission, though no basis for agreement was reached. Then, without a declaration of war, Japan struck.

The most charitable explanation is that even then this peaceful democracy did not comprehend the spirit that possessed the war-lords of the earth. If it expected a declaration of war, it certainly failed to read the signs of the times. The triumphs of Hitler had spurred the ambition of every military elite, for whom declarations of war were out of date. The Japanese had already made large conquests in Asia and the Southeast, and when Hitler invaded Russia they felt confident in planning bolder new successes. Incidentally, the deals between Hitler and Togo in the pre-Pearl-Harbor days make another revealing chapter in the diplomacy of deceit and miscalculation that reached its highest development in the Second World War. Hitler had wanted Japan to confine its adventures to the East and leave the Western world alone, but, committed by his ally and convinced that the United States would now attack Germany, he announced that Germany was at war with the United States. Italy in turn followed the lead. Now the war became truly global.

Already in the winter of 1941 the tide was turning against Hitler. The Russian winter and Russian resurgence took heavy toll of the German forces, and when in the following summer the latter again advanced—for the valor of the German troops was worthy of a far better cause—they were at length brought to a disastrous halt before Stalingrad. After considerable successes Rommel was thrust back at El Alamein. That remarkable leader knew when to retreat, but Hitler ordered him not to, causing the Germans serious losses. Hitler's intoxication with power, his belief in his infallibility, had already become a priceless asset to the Allies. In Russia, against the advice of his generals, he insisted on further advances, and when the devoted General Paulus was finally compelled to surrender at Stalingrad, to save from annihilation his starving and broken remnant, some 90,000 troops out of the 300,000 who had fought so bravely, Hitler poured his venom on the hapless commander, shouting that he and his men should have shot themselves instead for the greater glory of Naziism.

Now, under the supreme command of General Eisenhower, the Americans came into action, landing in Morocco and Algeria, and with the British occupying Tripoli the whole of Mediterranean Africa fell into Allied hands. After the seizure of Tunisia, the Americans and British invaded Sicily, and when the bombs began to fall in Rome the shattered Fascist facade collapsed and Mussolini was arrested without a shot fired to defend him. It looked like an ideal time for an Allied landing in the vicinity of Rome, but that landing came six weeks later in the Naples area, and there was much severe resistance from German forces before the Allies entered Rome.

During 1943 the growing revulsion in Germany against Hitler inspired a series of plots against him, all of which failed through miscalculation or fumbling. The mantle of the prophet and savior of his people had fallen off and revealed the misguided fanatic beneath. In one of these abortive plots Rommel was implicated. Hitler had him secretly done away with, followed by an official announcement that he had died of a hero's wounds. The military spearheaded the opposition to Hitler, for they could see the handwriting on the wall. Rommel himself had admitted that the Allies had achieved clear superiority "in the air, at sea, and on the land." And there was the great allied invasion of France now being mounted at the camps and the ports of Britain.

It is entirely reasonable to suppose that had the Allies at this time offered the German people decent terms of peace, terms of surrender that would allow them to rebuild their broken lives and create a new social order, while demanding stringent punishment for the great malefactors of that evil regime and such compensation as remained possible for those who were its victims, the war in Europe could have been ended far sooner. But the spokesmen of the two great democracies had offered nothing but "unconditional surrender," and if anything could have nerved the German people to fight on, with their memories of the previous peace, it was this gratuitous proclamation. Blood and suffering and horror called for vengeance on a people that, however misled, however responsible, had also had its fill of blood and suffering and horror—and even though the process of exacting this sort of vengeance would inflict on both sides and even on innocent third parties more and yet more blood and suffering and horror. And only a few years after the eventual peace, the Allies who had insisted on unconditional surrender were eager to help rebuild the Germany they had wanted utterly to destroy. Such is the wisdom of a power-focused world.

The mighty Allied invasion was launched at last, and began its long fierce march from the beachheads of Normandy to the banks of the Rhine and on toward Berlin. It was a tremendous assault as Americans and British and men from Canada and the other dominions and Frenchmen moved on through stubborn resistance and strong points all the way, while from the East the reinforced Russian armies advanced through Poland to the gates of Berlin. At length Germany's collapse was complete, and the prime author of its ruin, always a psychopath and now a near-maniac, screamed his last empty commands to shoot and shoot till the last German was dead on the field. The Russians got to Berlin first, by a prearrangement that was to cause grave headaches in later years to their wartime allies.

Meantime the Americans, with British aid especially in the Southeast, were closely engaged with the Japanese, having after some earlier vicissitudes severely crippled Japanese sea power. There was heavy fighting on the outer islands, notably at Iwo Jima and on Okinawa, and, under highly destructive bombardments of their cities and ports, the Japanese position became gravely deteriorated. The Allies made their regular demand of unconditional surrender, meeting with the usual lack of response. But, under conditions never before witnessed in man's history, the Japanese capitulated a few weeks thereafter.

All through the war years the industrially advanced belligerents bent their scientific and technological skills to the devising of yet more murderous weapons. The German scientists had invented the longer-range ballistic missiles, which caused some promiscuous destruction in London. "Improvements" were made in poison gases, and there was research in bacterial modes of wholesale slaughter. The use of these latter devices, however, ran into serious problems, not least the danger of a boomerang effect on the side using them. But the advances in atomic physics had raised the probability that the terrific power of atomic fission or fusion could be harnessed for human purposes, and its availability for controlled destruction was the object of the most intensive research by the best scientific brains. While many atomic scientists dreaded the consequences, in a world where folly so often prevails over wisdom, of the possession by mankind of so horrendously destructive a power, they knew that their German counterparts were working for the same objective, and it was of paramount importance that the Americans should reach it before the Germans.

There has been much controversy over the decision of President Truman to use the bomb against Japan. It is contended that the resort to so terrible a weapon, practically incinerating a whole city at one blow and spreading beyond it the insidious poison of its fallout, was a crime against humanity. It is also contended that the Japanese were already so seriously weakened that they would have shortly surrendered in any event. The former contention we must reject, though deeply conscious of the vast tragedy of Hiroshima and Nagasaki. All warfare is killing and mutilation, pain, disease, and sorrowing. Why then should the cataclysmic destruction of a bomb that cuts a war short be more deplorable than the more gradual ruination and the more protracted misery that otherwise would have taken place? Our argument, incidentally, has no relevance to the entirely different situation where more than one belligerent possesses atomic arms.

The only question here is how long it would have been before the Japanese were willing to yield. We do not know the answer. The Japanese were stubborn fighters. They had suffered grievous injury, but so had Germany and so had Britain and they both fought on. We do not know how many American soldiers and Allied soldiers and Japanese soldiers and civilians would have been killed or mutilated before peace would otherwise have come. And, not knowing, we can but regard the event as one of those terrible wartime decisions, on which so many lives depend, that the man in authority must always make.

There is, however, a different argument against the actual decision that cannot be lightly dismissed. Was there another practicable way in which the Japanese government could have been convinced that the Americans had achieved the final weapon and would use it to end the war unless Japan yielded? If for this purpose the bomb had to be let loose in Japan itself, could the demonstration have been made in some relatively desolate area of

that country? Then, had the Japanese government failed to be convinced, the awful responsibility would have passed from our government to theirs, and the outside world would have had evidence of our innate humanity. We do not know whether genuine consideration was given to this alternative. If it were given and the expedient was found unfeasible, it would be well to have the reasons fully stated. If it were not, then we must surely condemn the fateful decision made.

It was August 6, 1945, when the bomb fell on Hiroshima. Six weeks later the Charter of the United Nations was ratified. Thus were revealed the two potential bases for peace on earth, or at least for the deliverance of mankind from major wars. In 1945 men's hopes tended to center more on the United Nations, under whose Charter the two world powers and all the other nations admitted then or later pledged themselves to take appropriate measures for the pacific settlement of disputes, in order to save succeeding generations from the scourge of war. But power is not so easily tamed. In the Charter the signatories spoke of themselves as "peace-loving" nations, while the greater victorious powers regarded themselves as the joint guardians of the peace. It was highly significant, however, that each of these greater powers insisted on having the right of the veto, so as to remain the final sovereign arbiter over any decision that affected its "interests." And it was not long before the two great brothers-in-arms became bitterly divided and engaged in the perilous business of the Cold War against one another. So it has come about that such assurance as we have rests not on the love of peace but more precariously on the new dreadfulness of war, the prospect of sheer annihilation.

It is a remarkable fact, indicative of the cleavage that was developing between Russia and the West, that no peace treaty was concluded with Germany. At one of the earlier tries, Stalin demanded enormous reparations, which the Western Allies refused to accede to, but beneath that difference there was the major one that Stalin was already making temporary occupation a device for turning the occupied territories into Communist satellites. The last wartime conference of the Allies, at Potsdam, made some stipulations concerning Germany, including the prohibition of the production of materials and instruments for war, but this and later conferences got no further than the implicit understanding that the Western Allies organize governments for the territories they occupied while Russia did the same in the areas of its own occupation. The cleavage was already unbridgeable. As for Japan, the terms of surrender constituted the working basis of a settlement. Peace treaties were signed in 1947 with the other enemy countries—except Austria, which came later after one of the rare agreements between Russia and the West.

The upshot of it all was that Russia took the lion's share of the spoils, including on the one hand outright possession of the Kurile Islands, southern Sakhalin, territories on her western border, Bessarabia and northern Bucovina, and a Finnish port in addition to the Finnish territory she had previously seized, and on the other hand controls over Outer Mongolia and Manchuria, the occupation of Northern Korea and of the Eastern European states, including East Germany. Aside from some small border regions ceded by Italy to France, the other Allies made no important territorial gains. In this respect the United States took a particularly impressive stand.

Many of the concessions to Russia were the result of deals made at the Yalta Conference, where we sought to induce Russia to enter the war against Japan. At that time, in February of 1945, no one knew that within six months the war would be over in the

East as well as in the West. Against the tough bargainer, Stalin, Roosevelt felt he must make concessions for the sake not only of Allied goodwill but also of an earlier peace that would save many American lives. The Yalta agreements have been the subject of much controversy and bitter criticism. Perhaps Roosevelt, already a sick man, yielded too much. Perhaps some of the stipulations were not clearly enough defined. Certainly against so totally unscrupulous an operator as Stalin it was essential to leave no loophole of which he could take undue advantage. But how much of our hindsight should also have been foresight it is exceedingly hard to say.

When the East European states were assigned to Russia for postwar occupation, it was under an agreement that these countries would be restored to independence under free democratic elections. It has been claimed that here too there was a lack of clarity in the agreements, that Stalin put a different meaning on democracy, that he did not or could not understand what the Americans meant by it. This interpretation we consider quite wrongheaded. It was not a question of confused semantics but of deliberate violation of the agreement by a ruler who was as hypocritical as he was unscrupulous. There is no question about the meaning of free elections or of independence. There is no question that democracy has always meant a system of government under which the people in free elections establish a government of their own representatives. There are many questions concerning the realities of the democratic process and the conditions under which popular voting is effective, but these questions are not at issue here. The Polish people and the peoples of the other occupied countries were by agreement to be given the right through free elections to choose their own government—and that right was violated in every country and every territory under Russian postwar occupation. The fact that Stalin called the satellites under his puppet governments "people's states" with "real" democracy is merely an example of the perversion of language so characteristic of the regime.

Roosevelt was particularly concerned over the plight of unhappy, truncated Poland. He sent his special emissary, Harry Hopkins, to Moscow to plead with Stalin, but to no effect. So came about the historic irony that in one form or another has characterized the ending of more than a few wars. Poland was the country to save which from Hitler's tyranny the Second World War began, and when the victory was completed a diminished Poland fell under a new servitude to one of the victors.

5.

The Climactic Stultification
of Power

No great convulsion of the established ways settles into tranquillity when its thrust is spent. The upheavals, the wrenches, the cruel disruptions of the lives of men and peoples, the disruption of the firmament of habit and expectation, provoke a whole series of secondary commotions. To achieve a general settlement under these conditions, a basis not only for the restoration of stability but also for the attainment of some safeguard against the instability that was latent in the old order, demands no small degree of wisdom on the part of the inheritors of power.

Who, looking back over the postwar years, can doubt that such wisdom was sadly lacking? Instead the jealousies and ambitions of the victorious powers and the ruthless aggressions of one of them bedeviled and perverted the processes of the rebuilding of the shattered fabric of society across the earth. Cities were built, factories reconstructed and modernized, the ravaged countrysides re-ordered, trade was expanded, and science and technology brought newer gifts to mankind. On all levels of human endeavor—except politics, politics at the summit and politics on other levels, politics and the moral preconceptions of politics—the creative mind and the ingenious mind went forward, widening human horizons, increasing the resources of living, enriching the arts, advancing the battle against disease. Science, spurred by the demands of war, had opened up the tremendous potentialities of atomic energy, giving the promise of a future wherein the destitution that always hitherto had been the lot of the majority of men would be no more. Enormous though the physical destruction had been, it took only a decade or two to restore nearly all of the devastated areas—except for the priceless memorials and art treasures that were forever obliterated.

Nevertheless, at the end of these two decades, the greater powers were spending considerably more of the national incomes on preparations for war than they had ever before spent in a time of peace.

For this state of affairs we must attribute the heaviest responsibility to Stalin and his junta. It was they who thrust the first deepening wedge into the wartime alliance. Already bearing considerable responsibility for the Second World War, through the treacherous treaty they made with the war-ready Nazis in August, 1939, they now instigated the Cold War that, with its violation of pledges to liberate the countries under its control, its propagandistic attacks on Western "imperialism," its refusal to cooperate in American-initiated programs such as the Marshall Plan, and not least its promotion of guerrilla warfare in the new-rising countries of Asia against governments favorable to the West, has kept the world in turmoil and precluded any genuine peace settlement. The reaction of the West, led by the United States, to this hostility may not have been well-guided and certainly its leadership showed a lack of either initiative or distinction, but the onus for the Cold War cannot in the first instance be laid to its charge.

It may be that at Yalta the Western Allies were too ready to make concessions to the Soviet grasp for territory, and probably had they known how soon and under what conditions the war was to end they would have been more cautious. But at least they showed a spirit of accommodation, an eagerness to keep the alliance strong. And when the war was over the Americans, though they felt a more vehement dislike of Communism than perhaps any of the other Allies, had for the most part come to terms with the inevitable and were ready to maintain good relations with their big wartime partner. Their belief in the alliance was indicated by the vast and rapid reduction of the military establishment and of the expenditure on arms.

Even if the fear of "encirclement" by a hostile capitalist West still existed in the Soviet Union, feeding on Marxist doctrine and on remembrance of the ill-starred efforts of the Western Allies to bolster up the "white" generals in 1918 and 1919, no one could reasonably maintain that the security of the Communists was enhanced by what Stalin proceeded to accomplish, the total reversal of the spirit of alliance into one of seething distrust and increasing tension.

Stalin flouted his solemn and explicit pledges by setting up his puppet governments in all the areas of Russia's postwar occupations, in North Korea, in the East-European border states and— the deadliest blow of all—in East Germany. While the Western Allies greatly reduced their military forces in West Germany and elsewhere, the Russians kept massing troops around and inside their occupied territories. Stalin continued to demand exorbitant reparations from Germany, but the Western Allies wisely insisted that reparations should not be such as to prevent Germany from attaining a reasonably self-sufficing economy. On practically every issue there was nothing but the stalemate of complete dissension between Stalin and his recent allies.

Perhaps under no conditions could the relations between the two have been genuinely cordial. Only the urgencies of wartime and the formidable might of the common enemy had cemented the alliance. But a workable live-and-let-live agreement could still have been maintained in spite of the sharp opposition of the respective ideologies. Opposing ideologies have frequently enough lived side by side and at need have joined hand in hand. It was true that the Marxist ideology proclaimed the coming downfall of capitalism and the inevitable triumph of Communism. But that was to come about essentially through the spreading of the true gospel among the "oppressed" classes. The breach came not on that account but because the Stalinist mind was power-motivated. For it ideology was a weapon rather than an end. Stalin's outlook was jealous, vindictive, and brutal. To gain more power, to make his position absolute and secure, he had shrunk from no cruelty and no treachery. Engrossed by hatreds and by fears, he had no use for peaceful "coexistence." The Allied leaders, not least Roosevelt, were at fault so far as they trusted any of his pledges that stood in the way of his greater domination.

In the new consciousness of its role as a world power, the United States, faced with the task of upholding its position and its values against the stratagems, aggressions, and intensive propagandism of its world-power opponent, became for the first time immersed in global politics. One of the earliest and happiest of its endeavors to this end was the Marshall Plan, designed to expedite the recovery of the countries of Europe, and a year later, as the threat of Communism increased with the rapid communization of China and the growth of the Communist parties in France and Italy, it was followed by a major defensive alliance, the North Atlantic Treaty Organization. Thus was set the pattern of international relations during the postwar years.

The gradual revelation that the end of so calamitous a war was bringing not peace but a new intensive divisiveness had a very disturbing influence on the spirit of the postwar decades. Disillusionment became widespread, disillusionment concerning the future, disillusionment with the heritage of the past, disillusionment over civilization itself. After the First World War some aspects of the same attitude found expression in the works of writers and artists, as in *The Waste Land* and other poems of T. S. Eliot, in the brash iconoclasm of Ezra Pound, and in the more distorted human forms of Pablo Picasso's later pictures. But back of these manifestations there was often a revulsion from nineteenth-century "progress" and democracy to an earlier way of life, as in the cultural catholicism of Eliot or in the nostalgic orientalism of Pound. Whereas after the Second World War much of the newer literature and art seemed to reject all positive values, all the heritage of the past, in the mere depiction of anarchy and violence, of the reign of the "dark Gods" of the jungle —as suggested in the writings, say, of Norman Mailer and Saul Bellow, in the crazy quilt splashes of color beloved by certain artists, and in the murky plays of certain off-Broadway theaters.

Such exhibits were certainly symptomatic of the times, but we must not assume that they expressed the prevailing reactions. There is an artistic susceptibility that registers more intensively or more extremely the responses to situations that are manifested quite otherwise by the masses of men. People generally did share the sense of disillusionment, and a very large sector of them took it out in an accentuated fear, distrust, and hatred of Communism and all its ways. It was an attitude of which certain political figures took notable advantage.

The conditions that bred, or at least intensified, these reactions have continued with variations, with minor relaxations and renewed exacerbations, since the last great war ended in a never concluded peace. All the negotiations, all the diplomatic exchanges and summit meetings, all the proposals for disarmament and in particular for the abolition of nuclear arms, have been unavailing. For better or worse, people have grown more inured to a continuous state of international tension, and new alarms, new threats, new failures to end the impasse have made the sense of instability and suspense the background of their lives. From the Western point of view the situation was worsened when, after the unification of Red China and the retreat to Taiwan of the stubbornly ineffective Chiang Kai-shek, the new China, angered by American support for Chiang, manifested an even more aggressive hostility to the West than did Soviet Russia. The Western world responded to the challenge with massive rearmament, the strengthening of its defensive alliances for the Atlantic and the Southeastern areas, and measures of direct counteraction to maintain governments threatened by Soviet infiltration and guerrilla warfare.

More than anything else, because in its course it struck at the homes of so many Americans, the Chinese-inspired invasion of South Korea embittered the people of the United States against Communism and Communists. A United Nations truce committee endeavored at the outset to restore peace but found the new China adamant. The absence of the Soviet representative from the Security Council enabled that body to call on members of the UN to go to the aid of South Korea. Although a number of countries did furnish contingents, the United States bore the brunt of the ensuing war. In less than three months of severe fighting, the UN forces under General Douglas MacArthur had driven the invaders back above the North Korean line, the 38th parallel.

Here once more we meet the deadly instinct of war that is never satisfied when the initial objective for which it was waged is attained or attainable but must drive on to the consummation of victory, total victory or total defeat. It is true General Mac-Arthur called on the forces from North Korea to surrender at this juncture. But that is very different from offering peace, on the basis of the *status quo*. It implied Allied control over North Korea, and to that there was bound to be Communist resistance.

So MacArthur crossed the 38th parallel, driving into North Korea and nearly reaching the Manchurian border. The Chinese threw new troops into the struggle, the UN forces were thrust back, and Seoul taken by the invaders. UN overtures for peace were now rejected by the Chinese, and the dreary and bloody Korean War went on nearly two years longer, and for all the heavy sacrifices of these years the final peace was on the same basis as might reasonably have been looked for had MacArthur never crossed the 38th parallel.

The Korean War had an unhappy effect on the outlook of the American people, who had paid the major share of the price. On the one hand they had little interest in fighting to save South Korea, a remote unknown territory which stood for nothing in their eyes. The protracted war, when it seemed the first gallant rescue efforts had been in vain, accentuated their sense of disillusionment with international affairs, including the UN. On the other hand they regarded it, properly enough, as provoked by the wanton aggression of the Soviet powers. The resentment they felt against the provocative aggressions and betrayals of Communist policy now rose to fever pitch.

This situation was exploited by a number of petty power-seekers, who campaigned as champions of "Americanism," diverting attention from the very difficult problems the nation had now to face. They abused the function of the legislative committee by making it a kind of inquisition, accusing rather indiscriminately those who were "left of center" of being subversive or seditious or "pink" or "fellow travelers." Following the example of the House Un-American Activities Committee, various states set up their own investigating bodies. The House Committee itself held the center of the stage, followed at no great distance by the Senate Internal Security Subcommittee. Besides these public bodies, a number of private organizations, school boards, vigilante committees, and journals joined in the hunt. The spirit of the First Amendment was violated on all sides.

The period offered a particularly dismal exhibit of the abuse of power in a democracy. The Federal government disliked the business but was unready or unable to curb it. Many Congressmen disliked it but, fearing to lose public support, continued with the rarest exception to vote the appropriations of the House Committee. Senator Joseph McCarthy became the outstanding champion of "Americanism," making sweeping and indiscriminate charges in every direction. In the end he went too far, in his truculent attack on subversion in the armed forces. A famous televised investigation ensued, and his decline began when his public image, together with the flimsiness of his charges, revealed too clearly the quality of the man.

What made more serious these perversions of the democratic principle was that they beclouded America's major problem, which was how to combat effectively the challenge of a hostile Communist power that was skillfully exploiting the disturbances of the times. These disturbances were partly the legacy of the war and the unfinished peace, partly the consequence of the upsurge of nationalism in areas that had been colonial subjects of the Western powers. To meet this challenge it was essential to comprehend the source of the disturbances, to understand the aspirations and the needs of the peoples who were struggling toward independence and release from destitution, to provide them with well-planned material aid—for there are many ways of doing it ineffectively—to take their side, wherever feasible, against the feudalist rulers who sought to retain the *status quo,* and to present meaningfully the intrinsic worth of the democratic goal. Only exceptionally was this challenge understood and met. For the most part it encountered governmental inertia, routine performance, inadequate perception and planning.

The spurious outcries raised by the Communist-hunters were partly responsible. The way to combat the Communist assault was not to hound out of their jobs—unless in the rare instance where one might have access to information of genuine significance to a potential enemy—the small remnant of American Communists. Even so, the hunters were by no means content to unearth a hidden Communist here and there. All liberal and leftist tendencies were anathema to them. If an economist supported the doctrines of John Maynard Keynes—who was not only a brilliant thinker but also a director of the Bank of England and a successful capitalist to boot—he was following the road to Communist "serfdom" and ought to lose his position as a college teacher. If a young man with more idealism than experience and more imagination than knowledge took up the cause of Marxism in the first flush of its proclamation of a brave new world, but later had learned better and abandoned it, he was harried and publicized, and bidden prove his conversion by naming his associates of that earlier time, and cited for contempt if he refused. The House Committee compiled extensive lists of persons concerning whose "Americanism" it presumably had some question. Many persons of distinction in government, in public affairs, in arts and letters were on the lists. There was no redress against these wanton insinuations and charges, nor were there any judicial scruples in the methods and procedures of this and other investigatory bodies. They followed only too well the example set by the first Dies Committee, of which Walter Lippmann justly said that it became "a pillory in which reputations were ruined, often without proof and always without the safeguards that protect the ordinary criminal."

The furor abated with the decline of McCarthy, but the background conditions that made it possible were more deep-seated. There was the simplicity of mind that sees every issue as a sheer choice between God and the devil, an anti-intellectual bias fostered by a large proportion of the popular press, and the pseudo-patriotism that regarded all "socialistic" ideas as subversive. While there was some reform of the antijudicial procedures of the investigatory committees, they continued to operate with no change in their essential characteristics, and they still had the power to penalize people who had committed no offense deserving of punishment, as in the case of the elderly clergyman of New Hampshire who was sentenced to jail for a year because he would not divulge the list of the members of a World Fellowship Center he had set up and of which nothing blameworthy was known.

On the higher levels of government much concern but little leadership was displayed in the effort to meet the Communist challenge. The need to maintain our military strength on a level of high deterrence was realized, but the other important need, to combat Communism's acclaim of its own world triumph and its abuse of Western democracy as rapacious, imperialistic, and doomed to total decay, was very inadequately met. The United States in particular was under a serious handicap in its approach to the ex-colonial colored peoples of the earth. It was embarrassed by the persistence, not only in the South but across the whole country, of what was in effect a caste system relegating the Negroes and other nonwhite groups to a lower level of opportunity and excluding them from the residential areas and the social affairs of the whites. Still, the country could show a quite considerable improvement in the reduction of this disparity and a concerted action on the part of the Federal government, signalized by the 1954 antisegregation ruling of the Supreme Court, to combat this form of discrimination. So far as its attitude toward colonialism was concerned, its record was unusually clean. But at this juncture its appeal to the neutral and especially the ex-colonial countries was largely ineffective. Its effort was too exclusively occupied with attacks, not always well guided, on Communism, with aspersions on "Socialism," with generalities about democratic freedoms, and with laudations of "free enterprise." What was needed was a more constructive presentation, related to the conditions and problems of the countries to which it was directed and exposing the advantages of the more democratic way of meeting them. We failed to realize that poverty-stricken, capital-less countries must largely depend on socialistic measures in the earlier stages of their development, and that they certainly cannot become overnight or for a long time ahead full-blown democracies. Another weakness of our stand was the tendency to support in some instances feudalistic or autocratic rulers who professed to be on our side, when the revolutionary trend was moving their peoples to overthrow them —creating for us a really difficult problem.

There was one revolutionary situation that presented us with a different but peculiarly difficult problem, one we failed to solve, and when at last we resorted to the indirect use of mere power, we succeeded only in making our prospects hopeless. The Cuban revolutionary movement against *caudillo* Batista was on the whole sympathetically viewed by the United States, but when Castro won out we soon became thoroughly alienated. As a revolutionary leader Castro had eminent qualities, but once in control he became another kind of dictator, one with a Messiah complex. His confiscation of U. S. enterprises in Cuba, his refusal to give compensation for expropriated property, his wantonly exaggerated charges against the "Yankees," and his ruthless elimination of all who opposed his policies, led to bitter hostility on our part. At this time, for example, when he visited the United States, Castro was as yet by no means wedded to Communism. He was no devotee of any ideology. He was a revolutionary adventurer who, once he had seized power, was prepared to break his democratic promises and strengthen that power at any price. His indiscriminate seizure of lands and industrial installations was one method of increasing power and giving bigger jobs to the faithful. Always prone to identify as Communism any socialist regime, the United States treated him as a Communist enemy and thus helped to make him so. But Castro's doctrine was the purely emotional principle that what was good for the revolution and for his own power—the two goals were identified—was right. The United States was justified in protesting his uncompensated confiscations and his false charges, but what else to do, if anything, was the issue. It might have stopped there and presented its case to the

Organization of American States. Instead it began a series of severe economic reprisals, which inevitably had the effect of making Castro go begging for economic support from the Communist states.

This was bad enough, bringing about the first definite liaison between an American state and Soviet Russia. But worse was to follow. Most Americans regarded Castro's reiterated declarations that the United States was preparing to invade Cuba as just another of his wild charges. Unfortunately it proved to have a tragic element of truth. Banking on "information" purveyed by the Central Intelligence Agency, to the effect that the Cubans were ready to rise against Castro, the U. S. government secretly provided resources and training for Cuban exile commandos, and in due course the signal was given for the invasion. The result was a quick debacle for the invading force. Castro now proclaimed himself an out-and-out Communist. The United States suffered a heavy loss of prestige. Apart from other considerations, it had fomented and organized an attack to overthrow an established government, a course of action it constantly accused the Communists of following. But in politics what is sauce for the goose is not sauce for the gander.

On the world front the major historical problem of the exercise of national power had meanwhile manifested itself in its ultimate form. States had always been concerned to calculate the opposing power of other states when they went to war against them. An aggressor state reckoned, rightly or wrongly, on the potential superiority of its own side before it threw down the gage. Where there was manifest superiority on the other side, it might defend itself but it did not initiate a war. And there were times when relative peace prevailed over large areas because one power was supreme, as under the Pax Romana during the Roman Empire.

Similarly there might be a "balance of power" to deter aggressive war, as in Europe during the larger part of the nineteenth century when Britain with her superior sea power was an important influence in keeping the peace between two opposing alliances. But now, after Soviet Russia had mastered the secret of the atomic bomb—soon to be acquired by other powers as well—no calculation of superiority was any longer significant. So long as the great powers are so poised that a sudden atomic knockout blow by one of them on another would not prevent the deliverance of an annihilating retaliation from the other's wide-flung outposts no victory can ever be won, and warfare on the grand scale becomes the madness of mutual suicide, bringing ruin also to the rest of the earth. All the other powers are caught in the same net, because of the inextricable bonds of interdependence.

The only solution was glaringly obvious, but national power could not be expected to yield its ancient prerogative of the resort to violent enforcement without a stubborn struggle to retain it on some terms. The consequence has been a series of futile negotiations, nugatory summit meetings, protracted disarmament discussions, all the proposals and counterproposals, overtures and withdrawals that have occupied the rulers and the diplomats. The stalemate continued, with grandiose airy announcements of programs for world peace, threats, and occasional boasts of invincible power. The major and minor causes of dissension—the status and future of Berlin, the sovereignty claim on behalf of East Germany, the imbroglios in Laos and Vietnam, the Soviet demand for a tripartite UN Secretariat, and so forth—remained unresolved. The only answer to the dilemma of power, armament power too overwhelming and incalculably suicidal to be loosed—a secure agreement for the abolition of nuclear arms and a plan for the reduction to a mere policing minimum of all armaments—was bedeviled by dissensions and reservations. And meanwhile the powers continued to spend enormous sums in the search for ever more infernal engines of destruction.

Such was the stultification of power and the impotence of the strategy of power at which civilization arrived in the third quarter of the twentieth century, making this period one of peculiar significance in the nearer and perhaps in the longer history of mankind.

PART 2

THE GREAT
HISTORICAL TRENDS

NOTE FOR PART TWO

To appreciate the role of power in human society, to understand in particular the conditions under which mankind throughout the greater part of recorded history has been the instrument of irresponsible power, cloaked in authority and safeguarded by the indoctrinations, the rituals, and the usages sustained by the powerful, it is essential to explore on the one hand the nature of social power, with its numerous and very diverse manifestations, and on the other hand to trace the great historical trends that have shifted the residence, the distribution, the character, and the structure of the prevailing forms of power. In the process the role of functional power has been greatly enhanced and that of arbitrary power diminished, with consequences of great significance to social man. The process of transformation has now reached a crucial stage.

6.

The Ambit
of Power

Power is a many-sided thing. In its various forms and multitudinous expressions, it is the agent, indeed the very being, of all that happens on earth and over the whole universe. It is one quite particular form of power, power in human society, social power, that is the main object of our attention here. But it may provide more perspective, before we examine this form, if we consider the full concept of power itself.

All motion, all relationship, all process, all order, and all dissolution across the face of nature are expressions of power. Energy in its various manifestations, the radiant energies of heat and light, of cosmic rays, gamma rays, and the rays of longer wavelengths, the range of the electromagnetic spectrum, gravitation, and the forces operative or latent in molecules and atoms—this uncomprehended and still largely unexplored energy continuum —is responsible for all the incessant activity that moves in a spot of earth, in the mind of man, and in the endless reach of the galaxies. And now we learn that what we call matter is itself equivalent to a sum of energy.

In the human story energy, as the power to act, to think, and to plan, is equally primal, the agent alike of creative and destructive happenings. Power takes on a new significance altogether wherever consciousness develops. For now we enter the world of means and ends—a distinction unrecorded in external nature—of objectives and valuations, of wants and needs. Life wants to exist and to exist more abundantly. In this quest it learns to utilize the energies of its environment. In this quest, life becomes pursuit and struggle, conflict and cooperation, frustration and fulfillment. In this quest, power is the universal means, in all and over all, the road to every goal, the highest and the lowest.

At the first it was sheer necessity that impelled man to follow the road to power. Nature left human beings physically unarmed and unprotected by comparison with other animals. His flesh is not covered by hide or shell or other armor. He is without strong claws or fangs. He lacks the secondary protection of various unprotected animals, who make up for it by a capacity for rapid multiplication. This "forked biped" is at birth wholly helpless, unable to fend for himself, and he remains so throughout a prolonged childhood. And yet man has made himself the master of all other living creatures.

Herein we already see that power is not to be identified with physical strength or again with the physical means by which that strength is reinforced. Man is more powerful than the lion or the tiger because he has efficient know-how. He is Homo sapiens, the knowing one, the contriver, the manipulator. It is elementary in the first place that power is multiform, has many sources, and expresses itself in many ways.

By the possession of power we mean the capacity to control, regulate, or direct the behavior of persons or things. The power inherent in external nature regulates the universe, working in the laws all things must obey. The power possessed by man controls or commands the behavior of men and manipulates the energies inherent in things.

Let us review the sources of power in the human sphere and the manner in which they are utilized. First, we take *knowledge*. In its simplest usage knowledge enables man to rearrange and recombine objects. Primitive man, because of his more developed brain, his upright posture, free hands with opposable thumbs, and other attributes, was able to fashion sticks into spears, boughs into bows, stones into cutting instruments, and so to hunt and trap animals and to make rude utensils. He learned to collect the seeds of edible plants and sow them in earth he had turned over. Each learning led to new learning. By many stages he learned to manipulate and redirect natural forces, making his environment continually more serviceable to his ends, until he reached the present stage in which man has begun to harness the incredible power of the infinitesimal atom.

Knowledge is more than know-what, it is also know-how and know-when. In one aspect it is cunning, in another comprehension, and in the fullness of comprehension it becomes wisdom, for wisdom is knowledge guided by judgment, which in turn is the know-how and know-when as applied to decision-making.

Knowledge is power, but not merely power to manipulate and control material things. It opens up new goals, new opportunities, new choices, if also new temptations, new necessities, and new traps for our unwisdom. Above all, knowledge heightens our perceptions, enables us to make new distinctions, and enriches our understanding of the hitherto undreamed of marvels of the uni-

verse, opening the endless road of adventure and exploration, and
in the process liberating us from superstitions and the dark fears
of the unknown as well as from many positive dangers that otherwise could overtake us. Such is the power of knowledge, knowledge of the relations of things.

The process of knowing—learning, thinking, surmising, in-
quiring—is itself creative. It increases the lore that is our abiding
heritage and to which every generation contributes its quota. This
heritage is the foundation on which our arts and crafts are raised,
from the humblest to the highest, the source of our religions and
our philosophies, the stimulus of our aspirations. Ignorance is
weakness, knowledge the basis of our strength; no matter what
we seek, knowledge is a condition of our success. The ignorant
are unprotected against deluding hopes and misdirected fears,
against pitfalls and against exploitation, against disease and misery,
unable by themselves to acquire the material resources without
which there is neither security nor freedom.

Surely these are adequate reasons why we should place knowledge first among the kinds and among the sources of human
power.

There is another type of knowledge that is particularly difficult to acquire and the lack of which is a major explanation for
the miscarriage of other kinds of power. The first prescription of
the philosophy of Ancient Greece was "know yourself," but no
way was prescribed that would assure the attainment of this
knowledge. The sententious Tennyson elaborated the prescription
as follows:

> Self-reverence, self-knowledge, self-control,
> These three alone lead life to sovereign power.

Without some self-knowledge, we may certainly say, without the
judgment that duly assesses our own attainments and recognizes

the traps that our passions set for us, self-control must also be lacking, and the urgencies of ambition and power will end in shipwreck. The story of many emperors and kings and men of state corroborate the conclusion.

Knowledge guides to fruitful endeavor the other powers that lie within ourselves, the powers summed up in *personality*. Its various attributes, the quality of leadership, the strength of will, the bearing, the skill in presenting one's cause, and so forth, are in themselves and especially in their combinations important aspects of power. Weakness in one or more of such attributes will impair the efficacy of all the others and may even destroy it altogether.

From the internal we turn to the external determinants of power. These may be summed up in the word *possessions*. And these in turn consist of material goods, the power of ownership, and of social goods, the status or position one occupies and the milieu to which one belongs. These two forms are closely interdependent, though much more so in class-bound societies. In democratic societies one may acquire them both in various degrees, or being possessed of one may through it acquire the other to a considerable extent. In oligarchical or aristocratic societies, ownership of material possessions is mainly a function of birth and status.

To own anything substantial, whether on a temporary or a permanent basis, is to have power over its use. If it is land the owner can decide the manner in which it is utilized, choose his tenants or workers, and demand his share of the usufruct. Under feudal conditions the possession of land is the major condition of power, graded somewhat in accordance with its extent and its value-in-use. Ownership then confers a nearly absolute right, including political power as well as economic, and giving the landowner inordinate control over the lives of his tenants or serfs. The power of mere ownership has been considerably reduced in modern industrial society. Landownership lost much of its importance with the rise of capitalism, capital being versatile and capable of multiplication. The ownership of capital in turn became less potent as capital was concentrated into great corporate holdings the ownership of which is diffused among numerous persons and groups.

This latter change has greatly increased the role of *management*, making it now a very significant form of power. The scale of the modern corporation is vast, a single corporation sometimes employing an army of workers. The legal ownership, the body of shareholders, is too amorphous, too inexpert, and too remote from knowledge of the operations and the problems of organization to exercise practically any power over it. And there are interlocking directorates that magnify the power of leading executives.

Organization itself is a most significant source of power. "In union is strength" is as true as any saying can be. Competitive units can by uniting merge into a strong bargaining entity, perhaps the most notable example being the strength of modern trade unionism. Weak nations by joining forces can become a formidable power on the international scene.

From the power point of view, obviously the greatest of all organizations is the state, not only because it is sole repository of the power of physical coercion but because at need it can call on all the resources of the whole community, and because, while other organizations have limited power of control over limited areas of decision-making, the state has final regulative power over the whole range of human activity within it. The power of a government may be limited by constitutional law and by the will of the people, but the state itself includes the will that limits the power of government.

Mere size is no index of power, whether the size is that of the single unit or of the combination of units. The great unit may be cumbrous or unwieldy, top-heavy or ill-adapted to the conditions. So in the animal world the giant saurians lost out in the struggle with smaller animals that needed less food and made swifter attacks. So the great galleons of the Spanish Armada were harried and scattered by the nimbler more maneuverable English ships. So vast disjointed empires such as India and China were for long periods despoiled or conquered by the compact might of powers of smaller scale.

The various elements of power we have thus far distinguished, knowledge—skill or aptitude in any of its numerous applications —possessions, including external equipment of any kind—scale, management, and organization, combine into power complexes. The efficacy of a power complex is in turn increased or diminished by the various conditions under which it must operate.

Thus the impact of a great power complex is enhanced by the impressiveness it has for the human mind. Power carries an aura, a prestige, a glamor, or even an invisible halo that commands obedience in its own right. Great power surrounds itself with insignia, the panoply of office. At the summit of power, throughout the historical record, stands the king, the emperor, the dictator, the man of high estate, the supreme council. There are the trappings of scepter and sword, throne and great seal, court and ritual, symbols of the "divinity doth hedge a king," sanctifying power beyond the scrutiny of function.

The human mind pays tribute to the possession of power otherwise than by submitting to its commands. The great powerholder is looked up to, honored, at the least accorded some due of respect. Power has thus its own worthiness, its value-in-itself, in various degrees according to its extent and its effectiveness. It carries status, prestige, eminence according to its kind. This whole range of the impressiveness that makes power the more powerful we might designate as *authority*. In its stricter sense, however, authority signifies the possession of legitimate or invested power, associated with the fulfillment of function. But we also speak of the authority of persons who have made great achievements or acquired high distinction in any field. A great scientist, for example, has some authority among his brother-scientists and even beyond. A distinguished lady may have authority in the setting of fashion. In the words of Plutarch, "the mere nod of an esteemed person has more weight than a thousand arguments or expostulations from others." Authority is thus a source of power that may be a concomitant of function or may be entirely independent of specific function, as in the case of a sage, a man of rank, or, say, a former president.

We have touched here on a primary distinction within the area of social power, that between *functional* and *free* power. All organizational power is by design functional, that is, power assigned or recognized as requisite for or contributory to the fulfillment of some objective of the organization. Every form of social organization is integrated through a hierarchy of functions, a hierarchy that runs from the headman through a series of subordinates to the office boy. The respective power each member possesses within the organizational framework is derived from and presumably proportioned to the particular role or function each fulfills. He may, however, on occasion use this power freely, instead of functionally. When he does so in a manner contrary to the interests of the organization, we call it an *arbitrary* exercise of power. He may be motivated by other considerations than the rendering of service, by his private interest, conflicting obligations, by the promptings of his emotional or temperamental makeup. So he disregards his assigned role and employs his power in a manner contrary or irrelevant to his functional trust. It is an arbitrary use of power when, for example, he dismisses a good worker because he doesn't like his religion or the color of his skin, or when he prefers for promotion a less competent staff member over a superior one because the former flatters him or is a friend of the family. Such arbitrary distortions of functional power are frequent enough in every type of organization. They are, however, most notoriously exhibited in the various ranges of political organization, so much so that the spoils system, which discounts ability in favor of private economic or social advantage, is often openly practiced. The politician is usually avid for power and is tempted to regard it as a personal perquisite, to be used for his own aggrandizement. Moreover, the public interest, to serve which is his functional obligation, is so broad and so ill-defined that he can often disregard it with impunity or interpret it to suit his private interest. The public interest gets served in some degree—we will differ about the degree because we differ on the kind of service that is needed, but we can still agree that the efficiency of the service rendered is lower than could be achieved, did private or functionally irrelevant interests not intervene.

In the assessment of any power complex, the most important qualification is that power, no matter how seeming great, is limited or neutralized by opposing power. A small relatively unimpeded unit of power has more efficacy than a great amount of power that is negated by the resistance of strong opponents. When power takes the form of sheer force, its magnitude renders resort to it, in the face of strong resistance, very costly and quite precarious as an agency of policy. The extreme point at which the resort to armed might to achieve any end whatever becomes wholly irrational has, as we have already pointed out, been reached in the age of nuclear armaments.

In the modern highly organized society the foci of power are numerous, being kept in some kind of moving equilibrium by the incessant processes of conflict and cooperation. In a modern dictatorship the inevitable distribution of power within the system is hierarchically subordinated to the direct control of the central government, whereas in the democratic state the government is often called upon simply to be the final arbiter for the maintenance of order. It is therefore in the democratic industrial state that we see the full development of a restless swaying equipoise of freely striving interest forces, public and private, as they converge and separate over all the manifold areas of a diversified culture. There are endless impacts of organization on organization and there is ceaseless competiton between bodies with similar objectives, in such fields as religion and education and the performing arts, as well as resistances between bodies with dissimilar objectives, as at times between economic and political groups.

The above statement merely suggests the multiplicity and the complexity of the always partial interadjustment of powers that characterizes a modern civilization. One cannot contemplate this situation without realizing that power is an aspect of all the capacities of men, of their skills, their personalities, their persuasive arts, their resources of every kind, especially as these capacities are reinforced within the various organizations formed for the promotion of their respective interests.

The exercise of power is to a very great extent operative in other ways than through the mere resort to force or direct compulsion. The use of force can arrest, deter, divert activities, or at best clear the ground for new activities, but it cannot of itself achieve positive ends, it cannot of itself create or construct anything. There are, moreover, many gradations between the extreme of physical compulsion and the mildest suggestion that nevertheless carries enough weight or influence to be obeyed. Within the limits of indirect enforcement, there lie many sanctions that operate through the threat, overt or implicit, of the loss of privilege or gain of status or social acceptance. The Roman Catholic Church has powerful controls over the erring believer, in the last resort the sanction of excommunication. But that sanction is binding only because the faith itself is impelling. Even the armed might of a country, the outstanding exhibit of physical force, becomes ineffective where the people are disloyal and repudiate their allegiance to the government of that country. It is faith that in the end gives power to the sword. Other organizations, up to the state itself, can reject from membership, or preclude from the rights and privileges they confer, any member who violates its rules. The compulsion is the value to which the member clings. The danger of the loss of favor, promotion, patronage, or other prospective emolument, is again a strong deterrent against non-conformity. The fear of social ostracism is often a more effective control than the threat of a more direct penalty.

Any attribute that commands respect is in itself a power. We are usually ready to accept within his own field the verdict of a recognized authority, to heed his advice, to follow his directions. We are often influenced by the eloquent speaker, the persuasive exponent of a cause. We are more ready to respond to the wishes of a friend than of an outsider.

The doctrine that the state is essentially a power system has been proclaimed by philosophers and jurists and is still maintained in some quarters. This conclusion does not properly follow from the fact that the state, and the state alone, has the right of direct coercion. It is absolutely necessary that it have this prerogative in order to control crime, to ensure that order is maintained, to quell mob violence. But the final assurance of law and order is the loyalty of the people.

The conception of the state as preeminently might has been particularly applied to its external relations. It is the ancient doctrine of sovereignty, which in effect means that a state is of right free to act as it will toward other states. Here indeed the doctrine is seriously outmoded. It is associated with the dictum that war is an instrument of national policy. The "final argument of kings" or, as Dryden called it, the "trade of kings," was always a costly and often a ruinous recourse, but there have been signal historic situations in which it achieved great triumphs and won lasting conquests for the victors. Such situations belong to a vanished past. Major wars can never again win anything but desolation over the whole earth. Such war has ceased to be a usable instrument of national policy.

Military might still retains the highest place in the budgets of the great states, but for a curiously different reason—not to wage war but to prevent war from being waged. It is the logic of reciprocal fear, a logic that in the very nature of things can be only a temporary stage—unless reason is altogether dethroned on one side or the other.

Within the state the role of force is an entirely different one. We are here concerned with police power, not the power of armaments, with civil power exercised within an established order and operating to make it secure. There are times, under the rule of a tyrant or a ruthless insecure dictator, when the police power may become the mainstay of government, but in most states, even dictatorial ones, it is only the guardian of an order that is rooted in the active consent and cooperation or at least in the ready acquiescence of the people. This consent or acceptance is buttressed by habit, by indoctrination, by convenience, by interest, and by respect for what the government is or stands for. Moreover, the force at the command of the government, the force both of its military and of its civilian arms, depends on the will to serve, and behind it there is, if not the equilibrium of a party system, at least one party pledged to its support. It should be clear enough that the continued existence of government depends to a large extent on the will to maintain it.

To come to particulars, let us ask ourselves why *we* obey the laws. None of us, let us admit, obeys all the laws all the time. And when we don't obey, let us also admit, it is usually when we think we can get away with it. So we drive our cars faster than the laws permit and commit various other offenses where temptation and opportunity combine. Most of us are restrained from petty smuggling only by the fear of detection. And quite a number of us resort to various devices in order to underestimate the income taxes the law imposes on us. But there are thousands of laws we are all, in our respective roles, required to obey. And most of them we quite willingly obey, often without even being conscious of our obedience, while there are many offenses proscribed in the criminal code we would not dream of disobeying. It is not so hard to say why we disobey, but why we obey requires a more complex answer.

We have already suggested the lines of our answer, but let us elaborate it a little. We obey because we respect the code, even if we violate some of its demands. We obey because in one way or another it is to our interest to obey, because we want to be respectable and respected, because we don't want to set a bad example, because of mere inertia since to disobey would give us more trouble now or later, because we have formed the habit of obeying, because we fear either the penalties of violation or their indirect consequences. But we obey also because it is not only wise but also right to obey, because we have been trained in the virtue of law-abidingness and our conscience would be uneasy, in many situations, if we disobeyed. And on this ground we obey not only laws of which we approve but also laws of which we disapprove.

In the complex determination of law-abidingness the coercive power of the state certainly plays a role. But we should observe in the first place that the state exercises power over us in other ways than through the processes of enforcement. It influences our behavior because we are members of it, dependent on it, because it has benefits to confer on us, because its displeasure has serious social and economic disadvantages for us. In the second place various other determinants of our behavior than the power of the state, determinants rooted in our traditions, in our indoctrinations, in our conscience, combine to create the spirit of law-abidingness. Enforcement, lacking these strong bulwarks, cannot ensure our obedience. Only for the confirmed criminal, since he has abjured the sanctions of his society, are the penalties of the law the major consideration, and even so the fear of the law means not that he becomes less addicted to crime but that he is more circumspect in the planning of it.

Our object in this chapter has been to suggest something of the amplitude and magnitude of the ambit of power, which we so greatly underrate when we give primacy to one of its minor expressions, the compulsive power that violently interrupts the lives of men.

The incredibly vast universe itself moves forever in subjection to its laws, the primal order expressed in the balance of attraction and repulsion. Matter itself is equivalently power, cohering in exact obedience to its immutable laws. So too in the little wonderland of human life on earth power is still the fulfillment of law. But man has himself a special power, the capacity to manipulate the law-ordered forces of nature and to direct them to serve his own ends. He cannot violate the laws of nature, but, when he has superior power over other men, he is subject to temptations that lead him to misuse this power in ways that cause much disorder in society and sometimes bring disaster to himself. It is the conditions and the problems of such an abuse of power that will presently occupy us.

7.

Power and
the Creative Mind

Power, as energy, is the primal reality, the actuality of all being. But there is one manifestation of energy, the energy called life, that exhibits remarkable differences from all other forms. Life is awake; all other energies are locked in eternal unknowingness. Being awake, becoming more awake, it is aware of itself and of its special world. Becoming more awake, it becomes free in a sense in which nothing else in the universe is free. Its freedom is its consciousness of alternatives of action, of at least apparent choice between alternatives. Life is a unique form of energy, of being. We cannot fathom the difference, we know only the ways in which it expresses itself. We say life is creative, capable of developments beyond the power of prediction. One of its uniquenesses is that it learns to become in degree master over other energies, in the sense that it can utilize them for its own expression. Life is forever seeking, wanting, needing, building, destroying, and rebuilding. The self it endeavors to fulfill reveals its nature only in the modes of its expression, in the weaving of relationships with its environment, with other selves, even with the dreamlike simulacra of its own imaginings.

In lower organic nature the creative processes have begun to stir. In the vegetative world it is no more than a stirring in a sleep, expression of which there is no awareness, the unfolding of the plant, the reach toward the realization of a form, the genetic urge that evolves the spore or the seed and provides for its germination. In the animal world the senses awaken, perception advances, and new creative processes begin, as the animal devises techniques for hunting its prey and for avoiding the predator, digs its burrow in the ground or builds its nest in the tree, elaborates the formulas of mating, registers emotions with its voice, stores its winter food, joins in companies for greater assurance or efficiency, and so on through innumerable variations. But the creativity is mostly limited within the satisfactions of self-preservation, reproduction, and protection of offspring. Going little further, it conforms to repetitive patterns of what we call "instinctive" behavior.

In the growing child we follow the development of the creative urge toward new plateaus of aspiration. At first the immediate animal cravings for food, warmth, comfort, protection engross the wakening senses, but gradually there supervenes an awareness of social and emotional needs, of developing capacities, and the urge toward freer and fuller expression. New interests take hold as horizons widen. After a period that is mainly imitation of the ways of grown-ups, the child's own habits take shape. The power of speech increases and enables the individual to assert the more his own individuality, not infrequently with resistance to the pressures of the elders. The youth wants to feel his power, his selfhood in action. His personality is already manifest, and the extent to which it will become richer and fuller depends alike on his native endowments and on the opportunities and incentives his environment provides. Adverse circumstances may thwart him, poverty may cramp him, his own temperamental difficulties combined with parental mishandling may drive him to assert his independence in wasteful and unrewarding ways. One way or another the creative urge seeks outlet, even if the outlet is no better than misdirected rebellion. Always the growing youth seeks something more, something different from what he yet is or has.

What an arresting picture we would see if we could comprehend the whole spread of the life urge over the members of a growing generation—the myriad individualized power drives of youth pushing, scheming, striving to find itself, pursuing a thousand directions, seeking its way through the niches of the society that sustains and limits, advances and baffles and defeats its efforts! Ambition may be misguided or excessive, aspiration may be faulty or perverse, and, through lack of understanding, emotional skewing, or too congenial distractions, the direction pursued may lead not to achievement but to frustration. Power without knowledge or without discipline is almost inevitably destructive, even where its aim is to construct.

Power always wants to be free but often misunderstands the conditions of freedom. Freedom of action, which is almost a synonym for power, is demanded by the creative urge of youth, and, when the demand is not controlled by the sense of responsibility, it becomes the enemy of the freedom of others as well as baleful to its possessor.

We often nowadays speak, usually by way of contrast, of a free society, a free people, and often enough we use the expression loosely. A free society is one so ordered that it gives the freedom of opportunity to the creative urge in its members so far as in using it they do not inflict positive injury on their fellows. It is a society in which authority is held responsible so that it will not abridge certain fundamental rights or liberties that are constitutionally guaranteed nor permit any citizens or groups of citizens to violate them.

There is thus a profound difference between the distribution of power in a free society, a democracy properly so-called, and in a dictatorship or an oligarchy. The difference lies in the range and the quality of opportunity that is given to the creative urge. In the democracy the highest forms of the creative spirit, in religion, in the arts, in literature, in philosophy, are wholly liberated from the coercion or the corraling of governmental authority, whereas the totalitarian principle makes them the kept servants of the state. In the dictatorship, science is stimulated and honored, but even there the jealous state may find that a particular conclusion or theory is contrary to the dogma. Only technology, the utilitarian child of science, is given wholly free range.

Where government is all-powerful the citizens are cramped in the exercise of the greatest of all liberties, the liberty of the mind, and with this deprivation all their other liberties are reduced. Where the power of government is limited and made responsible, voluntary associations of many kinds have their own autonomy, and everyone, high and low, has "the liberty to know, to utter, and to argue freely according to conscience." We must make certain minor reservations to that statement, partly because no democracy is wholly true to itself, partly because it is desirable that citizens should be protected against assessable damage from unguarded utterances. So we have laws against slander and libel and against deliberate incitement to violence. On the other hand there are failures of particular private associations and of individual powerholders to respect the reasonable freedoms of their employees or dependents. And sometimes a democratic government, through some of its agencies, betrays certain liberties its mission should be to defend, as happened notably in the emotion-ridden days of Senator Joseph McCarthy. But these limitations do not seriously affect the vast distinction between a democratic system and a dictatorial one.

The way in which an organization is structured has an important bearing on the distribution of power within it, on the degree to which its various members, whether staff or employees, can respectively find within it some scope for their creative impulses. There are, for example, strongly hierarchical types of organizations that put severe limits on the initiative of their members. A military organization is usually regarded as the most hierarchical of all types. Orders are passed down the line and call for precise obedience in accordance with prescribed routines. "Theirs not to reason why" might be taken as the primary requirement of the service. But in some respects this is an outmoded model. Blind obedience to simple clear-cut orders may have sufficed when armies moved as compact masses, in serried ranks. But modern strategy must conform to modern technology, and thus demands not only a considerable variety of differentiated skills but also a degree of initiative, an ability to size up situations and adapt oneself to constantly changing and unforeseen developments, when, for example, communications may be disrupted. In consequence, while the necessity of thorough discipline is still recognized, there have been important modifications of the training process, calculated to prepare even the rank-and-file soldier to meet conditions as they arise. Thus even in the ancient strong-hold and exemplar of the principle of unthinking obedience its gross inadequacies have become apparent.

It is hard indeed to conceive of any kind of organization in which the suppression down the line of the creative play of the mind is not detrimental to the service rendered. It used to be a complaint within certain large-scale government departments that operations were so routinized that the bright younger men were given no chance to show their quality. The writer himself recalls a period when some of his finest doctoral graduates entered certain governmental departments with high zeal, to leave them after a year or two because the rigorous demarcation of their tasks gave no outlet for their training or capacity but instead made them mere scribes and précis writers conforming to a pre-scribed pattern. This evidence, we hasten to add, refers to con-ditions some decades ago and has no necessary implication for the present time.

Some organizations are hierarchically constructed because their functions and objectives require it. They are usually sys-tems in which a strict discipline, a readiness to face emergencies, an immediate responsiveness to commands are called for. In such systems, however, it is often a mistake engendered by the power complex of the top brass that simple, almost mechanical obedience is the whole duty of the underlings. The writer has known a police department that some time ago had a headship inclined to this viewpoint. Consequently, at that time the training of the policeman on the beat provided little guidance on how to deal with situations in which alternative actions were available to him. Actually, every policeman and every officer up the line must use discretion under quite a variety of conditions in the choice between such alternatives. One type of situation arises, for example, when a policeman has to deal with youths who have fallen into some minor trouble with the law. Quite frequently he has the alternative of warning the offender and letting him go, settling on the spot some simple complaint against him, deciding, in conjunction with the precinct officer, that he should be brought to court or be referred for further investigation to a special youth division of the police. If he is untrained he may resort to rough-and-ready methods, without serious consideration of the nature of the problem. He may even get to think that the only power he possesses is the power of the nightstick and so fail to develop at all the important power that lies within his area of discretion.

In the business world, organization tends to be more flexible, more subject to change, which occasionally takes a quite drastic character. The personality of a few strong men, or even of a single autocrat at the top, makes a marked imprint alike on the efficiency of the business and of the scope for initiative in the subordinates. Sometimes the role of the workers, especially in areas of highly automatized operations, may seem to be purely mechanical and routine, stamping with a die, moving a lever up and down, pushing a button, and so on. But even here some discretion is called for, not merely to mitigate the monotony of the task, but for effective operation. There is a matter of timing, of checking, of precision, of the quick eye that spots early signs of trouble. Actually any purely repetitive operation is ripe for the machine to take over. The more the machine can take over, the less purely mechanical becomes the control function of the worker. Let us admit that all regular labor tends to get somewhat monotonous, but let us also remember that mechanical toil is less wearing than the older heavier forms of drudgery. Moreover, mechanized operations involve divisions of labor within a chain series of services, and this makes the more feasible and the more desirable a plan for consultation and discussion of procedures between the workers of various kinds and their superiors. Through such opportunities for reporting on the conditions and problems of their tasks and for making suggestions for improvements, the workers are no longer treated as hands but as men, and thus receive an additional incentive on the job.

Everywhere one encounters the contrast, greater or lesser, between the more rigidly authoritarian and the more flexibly integrated form of organization. Everywhere we find also the tendency of some within the organization, of whatever rank, to dominate and reduce the reasonable and efficiency-promoting powers of others for the greater power of themselves. We observe these contrasts alike in factories, trade unions, churches, ecclesiastical systems, in all areas of management.

The conception of the character and the role of power differs in the opposing types. In the authoritarian type, power is treated as a virtue, as a good-in-itself, not merely as a means of obtaining or of doing desirable things. The stress is laid on power as enforcement, the strong hand, the iron will, the succinct clean-cut command. The concept of discipline is reduced to that of mechanical obedience. The organization becomes the vehicle of a personality, the embodiment of his will. "The state, that's me," said Louis XIV. There is contempt or hatred for opposition. "Take away that bauble," rapped out Oliver Cromwell, as he pointed to the mace that signified parliamentary authority, when he dissolved the relic of the old Parliament. The creative spirit, struggling, reflecting, probing, is given little play for development, has little esteem. There is more trust in intuition than in the slower processes of discovery. The variant proposals of others are given little consideration. The doctrine, the program, the blueprint of the powerholder are without question always right. For the authoritarian type, accommodation to changing conditions, to unanticipated snags in the execution of orders, and unanticipated results when they are executed is difficult, disturbing, and grudging.

In the flexible type, power takes on a wider significance. The importance of initiative is admitted not only at the top but on every plane of operation. It is signified by the relative autonomy assigned to departmental heads, who are assessed more by their ingenuity and discretion in promoting the interests of the organization than by their mere faithfulness in carrying out orders. The general policy is to enlist as far as possible the cooperation and the sense of participation in a common purpose in staff and workers alike. In the flexible type, there is more willingness to permit the expression of dissent, to pay some consideration to criticism of procedures announced or already put into operation by the top management. The leadership is more concerned to elicit loyalty to the organization than a chorus of agreement over its every procedure.

The broad distinction between authoritarian and flexible types of organization is signally illustrated in the contrast between democratic and dictatorial governments. By its very constitution a democracy not only tolerates conflict of opinion but actually depends for its existence on it. Without interparty conflict no democracy could continue. Every democratic government must, during its term of office, face and answer the constant attacks of at least one opposing party, and this condition has a salutary effect in restraining the dominating tendency of power.

Under a democratic system, should a member of the cabinet or a high-placed servant of the administration resist or denounce the policy he is under obligation, while in office, to support, he may resign without any diminution of his civil rights and then continue to oppose the government. When, for example, President Harry Truman, in his role of commander in chief, recalled General Douglas MacArthur from his Korean command because of the latter's opposition to the military policies of the administration, the demoted general on his return was greeted with the acclamation of parading throngs. In a dictatorship such as Soviet Russia, he would have been at least relegated to silent obscurity, no voices raised on his behalf, and would count himself lucky not to be "liquidated."

Between religious organizations we find in degree the same contrast. Some insist on a strict orthodoxy, with clean-cut theological formulas and a code of behavior spelled out to cover many contingencies. The creed and its applications are interpreted by the church, and its official proclamations are issued as guidelines for changing situations. Heresy is roundly condemned, and members who persist in heretical notions or in disobeying the church ordinances are cast out from the fold. Others are more tolerant or lax about doctrinal differences, but demand strict observance of a moral code, usually of a puritanic character, tabooing practices that are in vogue in the world outside, such as taking alcoholic liquors, dancing, and card-playing. Some lay down particularly strict rules about the relations of the sexes. Some are specially insistent on ritualisitc observances, with fasts and feasts, dietary rules, set times for prayers, and so forth.

In this area we have the best examples of a form of power, exercising direct controls over considerable members, that is inherently inconsistent with direct coercion. Some church systems have, it is true, exercised political or "secular" as well as religious authority. The medieval Roman Catholic Church claimed and at times possessed the "two swords," the secular and the spiritual, and in the confusion of faiths in the following centuries both Protestants and Catholics suppressed where they could the opposing religion and otherwise exercised not inconsiderable political powers. All this was another illustration of the manner in which power, power of any kind, seeks to expand itself. The arrogation of political controls by a primarily religious organization is intrinsically dangerous, because the power drive stimulates motivations and interests that tend to pervert the religious attitude. It proved also to be socially disruptive in situations where peoples were divided in their religious affiliations, breeding wars and persecutions, until the time came when the sheer necessity of national unity led people to realize that citizens of different creeds could live together in peace.

In passing we note that the exercise of coercion in the name of religion is a peculiarly flagrant and arrogant abuse of power. It rests on assumptions that outrage the soul of religion—"not by might but by my spirit," as the great doctrine says. It assumes that you can compel people to believe. It assumes that you should punish, torture, or kill people because they cherish different beliefs from yours. It assumes that any organization dedicated to religion can remain uncorrupted and still engage in the hurly-burly of power politics. Only the inordinate drive of power could lead anyone of decent intelligence to credit such childish notions.

Nonhierarchical religious systems, whatever their limitations, are at least less prone to abuses of power. They do not regard difference of opinion over the interpretation of a creed as heretical or a refusal to accept some pronouncement of a church assembly as a ground for denying membership. They do not have any elaborated theology. Some are so unhierarchical that they leave their congregation free to pursue their separate ways within the rather loose bond of a body of ethical principles. Indeed, it is rather hard to distinguish religious organizations of this type from ethical societies or schools of ethical thought. We think, for example, of Confucianism as a religion, but it lacks orthodoxy and the ecclesiastical bonds that are characteristic of the historical churches of the West.

Obviously the less control a church exercises over the beliefs of its members the more liberty the latter have to adapt the faith to their own temperaments and standards. This may spell either indifferentism on their part or some degree of "liberal" thinking. Where a strict orthodoxy is prescribed, the church member presumably accepts implicitly the injunctions and inter-pretations officially delivered—though there is a considerable amount of evasion and merely formal acceptance. Since to doubt is to sin, the true believer of an orthodox faith, if he has an active mind, limits his speculative tendencies to discovering new significance in the prescriptions of the faith or to expounding and illustrating its applications to particular problems of the times.

The more hierarchical the religious organization is the more it is likely to make its impress felt on the political as well as on the social life of the community. Some authoritarian churches, notably the Roman Catholic, are frequently active as discrete pressure groups in various areas of legislation, to a considerably greater extent than the less unified and less authoritarian churches.

We have dwelt on the power tendencies of religious bodies, because they offer so striking a historical demonstration of the problem of relationship between two kinds of power, political power with its inevitable aspect of enforcement, and spiritual power understood as working through indoctrination, persuasion, and interpretation, depending in no way on enforcement but appealing directly to the mind.

Over the whole area of the cultural life we find the same

problem. It is exhibited, for example, in the educational field, in school systems, colleges, universities. The school usually lays down more specific regulations concerning the teaching process and the behavior of both students and teachers than does the institution of higher education. The difference is at least partially explained by the fact that the school has charge of children and must assume in some measure the role of guardian or surrogate parent. It is noteworthy that it is the universities and colleges of the highest standing that show least tendency to impose administrative controls on the initiative of their teachers. State institutions in this country are subject to legislative controls, imposed through the power of the purse, that may override the policies of the educational administrators, though there is great variation in the degree and in the manner in which such controls are applied. Church-affiliated colleges and universities impose a different form of control, since they are concerned that the attitudes and viewpoints of their teachers are not out of accord with the tenets of their religion, though the extent of such control depends on the degree of authoritarianism characteristic of the religious organization.

The contrast between the more authoritarian and the more "liberal" holds not only for organizations as wholes but also for their various divisions and departments. In institutions of learning, for example, the head of one subject department chooses for colleagues and assistants men who adhere to his own school of thought and are ready to echo his ideas and to feed his pride, regardless of whether men of higher scholarly attainments but more independent attitudes are in consequence kept out of his domain. The head of another department seeks out the most able associates he can find and gives them free rein to pursue their own researches and reach their own conclusions. Within the

school system, again, we find one principal who insists on prescribing to the letter the lessons the teachers have to give, cramp-
ing thereby their initiative and their ability, whereas another
encourages the teacher, within the limits of the curriculum, to
evoke in his own way the capacities and the interests of his pupils.
The power drive is concerned, first and foremost, with the aggrandizement of its possessor, no matter how that objective may
skew the performance of his function.

Wherever power is directed mainly to the imposition of one's
will on others, the conception of the nature and the value of
power is narrowed to its more primitive form, to its more external
and ruder expressions. In magnifying the person it distorts the
personality. To magnify the person it suppresses the personality
of others. So far as it creates, it is to exhibit magnificence, display, bigness, or to achieve triumph or conquest, small or great.
It can build vast monuments to itself, like the mausoleum for
the bones of Mausolus or the moldering pyramids that stand in
the barren sands of Egypt—but this piled labor of myriads of
slaves is no contribution to the culture of mankind. Rarely
enough, the man of power possesses and retains the creative
spirit, so that his power is animated by a greater purpose. So,
for example, did Julius Caesar, mighty and sometimes ruthless
conqueror that he was, work to build a great liberal civilization
within the empire he so greatly expanded, united under the "law
of nations," while he readily granted the freedom of Roman
citizenship across the imperial possessions. Thanks to such constructive measures and the Roman genius for liberty under law,
the empire he so greatly expanded not only endured for many
centuries but, in spite of the follies of later emperors, contributed
culturally to the upbuilding of great new nations reared upon
the foundations Roman civilization had established. The power

of empire, like all power resting on domination, must at length dissolve, and what it bequeaths depends on the creative forces that entered in the train of power, the crafts and the lores, the skills that construct systems of order and modes of thought. So it is today with the vanished empires that the British, the French, the Spanish, and other conquering peoples built.

In an earlier chapter we commented on the fact that military power has become too monstrous to be employed by the great nations in warfare with one another. For a totally different reason imperial power has also become outmoded. No empires in the old sense can take the place of those that have so rapidly crumbled in recent decades. The spread of the spirit of nationalism, the rise of a multitude of ex-colonial nations fiercely opposed to imperialistic designs, and their new ability to win to their side one or other bloc of great powers jealous of encroachments by the opposing bloc, suffice apart from other considerations to restrain new imperialist aggressions.

To sum up, the place of large-scale physical enforcement in human affairs, of the power of nations to impose their will on others by direct coercion, the simplest most primitive form of power, has greatly diminished in recent decades. Enforcement has still a significant and necessary role, but mainly as the law-sustained police power. Actually, the role of force, especially of military might, has generally been overestimated as an explanation of the course of human history. Force appeals to the untutored imagination, because it produces the most immediate, the most spectacular, as well as the most convulsive results, and in our traditional history books it has occupied the center of the stage. Happily the tradition is now changing. We must give priority to the long-term forces that have built the kind of world in which we live, to the quietly creative urges that express themselves in our cultural heritage, in our scientific advancement, and in our ceaselessly developing technology. To such we owe our outlook on the world, our modes of thought and of speech, our protection from epidemics and from various diseases that ravaged our ancestors, our resources and amenities of living, and the new energies that have already reduced and now promise to abolish altogether at length the destitution that has hitherto been the lot of the great majority of men. These results live on while the "dreams and tramplings" of conquest have become mere echoes of a buried past. The scientist, the great teacher, the poet, the artist are in the longer perspective

> . . . the movers and shakers
> Of the world for ever, it seems.

8.

The Primacy of Knowledge
as Power

Thomas Hobbes, when he pondered over the question how government first arose, concluded that, men being so nearly equal, no one of them could in the "state of nature" have gained authority over a whole tribe or people by his own strength or resource. Yet in every society one man or one little coterie of men were the rulers over millions. He could see no way it could possibly have come about except through a kind of agreement or covenant. Men are weak creatures, unarmed by nature, and their differences in ability or in prowess are mere variations around a mean. They are also envious, quarrelsome creatures, and that meant a state of affairs in which every man's hand was against every other man's, with endless promiscuous strife that defeated every hope of betterment and made life for everybody "poor, nasty, solitary, brutish, and short." At length they found the only way out of their wretchedness by agreeing to surrender their "natural rights," their little powers to do as they pleased, to "one man or assembly of men," who would lay down laws to govern them all.

Hobbes was an exponent of the doctrine that makes the sheer power of enforcement the end and the being of government. It is a doctrine that is still championed today, in more sophisticated forms. In all its forms it underrates the manysidedness of power, the complexity of the controls and influences to which human beings are responsive.

The power of man over man has existed from the dawn of society. It is rooted in the relation of parents and offspring, in the life of the family and the kin group, parents ruling over children, the seniors over the juniors, the patriarch over the kin. It was never mainly a question of physical strength. Authority was inherent in the very nature of society. Seniority was buttressed by indoctrination and training, by the know-how of greater experience. The teaching of the elders developed into the tribal lore, and the tribe became a close-knit unity. The older-established families had more authority than the later-established. They engrossed the better lands, the larger properties. The rules of family inheritance accentuated social distinctions. So a governing elite arose, and among them some had qualities of leadership, perhaps more aggressiveness or more cunning, and became chiefs and sages, the men of power.

Power, the power that rules the world of men, exists only within a system of relationships. It is not an attribute men possess apart, in themselves, like, say, industriousness or zeal or muscular strength. Nor is it like a gift that can be handed over to you intact, like, say, a sum of money. You can have bestowed on you not a sum of power but a *potentiality* and an opportunity that depend for their power worth on the possessor's personal qualities and on the situation in which these have to be exercised. You can be given position and status. You can be heir to a throne. But some kings have been weaklings and came to naught, and some have been fools and accomplished nothing except failure. Louis XIV was a mighty monarch, Louis XVI lost his throne and his head. And there have been kings who were themselves ruled by an astute statesman or even by a clever courtesan. They had the potentiality and the opportunity, but they lacked the know-how to rule.

Hobbes the individualist failed to understand the social implications of power. He thought of power itself in very narrow terms, the force that keeps men in subjection. Those who extol sheer force have a tendency to think in Hobbesian terms, especially when thinking of national sovereignty and its role in international relations. Carlyle, for example, was a great admirer of power in this sense, and of the strong men like Frederick or Napoleon who could make that power felt. Correspondingly, he liked to depict the weaknesses and follies of the lesser men who made pretensions to power. In one passage he drew a picture of some big ceremonial affair, imagining that suddenly the clothes flew off the whole assembly and they were revealed as posturing whitish "forked radishes," so to speak, cutting a ludicrous figure when the borrowed plumes, the uniforms, the insignia, and the resplendent costumes were removed. The race of men is ready to be dominated by the man of iron.

The very word "power," unless qualified by an adjective, accents the notion of forcefulness, might, dominion. We speak of nations as powers, referring to their size, resources, and above all military strength. But power, the power that in its more eminent manifestations moves and transforms the world, the power that is in the longer run the maker of history, must be thought of in more subtle and more complex terms. Power, on the human level, means capacity for effective action, and the quality and scale of action depend on the utilization of resources through the requisite skill or art, the knowing that includes know-how, know-what, know-when, and know-where. The knowing is primary, for that knowing itself can sooner or later possess itself of the resources it needs.

Every worthwhile achievement is triggered and directed by knowledge, and, though it has always been the fact, it is only in our own times that the high significance of widespread knowledge even for military strength has become properly recognized. Soviet Russia rose in the course of two or three decades to become one of the two world powers, not because of its Marxist ideology but because it brought education to the deprived masses and concentrated on the nationwide development of technology, the know-how. He who possesses in high measure the aptitude for all-round knowing and the will to follow it through becomes a master among men. A being who possessed it in supreme measure would thereby be a God.

The remarkable myth in the Genesis story of creation concerning the fall of man has a curious significance. Adam had all the joys of the Garden of Eden so long as he refrained from eating the fruit of the tree of knowledge. If men ate the fruits of knowledge they would "be as gods, knowing good and evil." They were safe and happy so long as they did not possess that double-edged power. And it was the devil who tempted Eve to take the fruit of the tree.

The fear of knowledge, the atavistic sense that knowledge is perilous, that the knower, conceived of as the wizard, the medicine man, the dealer in magic possesses power to do them harm, to put them under a spell, blight their crops, strike them with diseases, is common among the simpler peoples. They live in a world of natural perils; the storm, the flood, the lightning, the drought, the terrors of the night, the pestilence, they are equally the work of the dark spirits that send them forth. The magic of the knower may be able either to invoke or to control these manifestations, but is more likely to invoke them.

Some distorted echoes of that ancient fear persist into our own times. In some quarters the intellectual is looked on with suspicion and even dislike. It is an ambivalent attitude, for he is regarded as impractical, a theoretician who knows many things but not the things that matter. It may not be without significance that the only profession that is not permitted to direct its own institutions is the academic. The highbrow is not to be trusted, especially when he ventures into politics. There is an anti-intellectual bias that prefers the cheap folksy go-getting politician to the man of ability.

People in general grossly underestimate the primacy of knowledge over the long process of human advancement. The history books we used to read turned the past of mankind into a tale of kings and conquests, heroes and treasons. The great forces that formed and changed the face of society, and the men who liberated them, the thinkers and artists and prophets and poets and inventors and scientists, received scarcely a mention. In our own days physical science has gained a new esteem among the people, though mainly because it produces such practical results, not because it has changed and widened and enriched the thoughts and ways of men. Another area of science, the sciences of man himself, is still looked on in many quarters with misgivings. So they have been slowed in their development. The same strangely liberated Greek whose first injunction to his disciples was "know yourself," also thought that virtue was knowledge, the knowledge of the due proportions in the relationships between man and man, the knowledge of what his great successor Aristotle called "the golden mean," the balance between excess and defect.

The viewpoint of Socrates that virtue was knowledge is most instructive, if we are willing to scan its significance. Let us first premise that the word we translate "virtue" stresses excellence and manly quality, unlike the narrowly moralistic connotation the word has generally for us. And knowledge meant no cold formal learning, but the rich understanding of the relationships of things. While any kind of knowledge can be serviceable to virtue, one kind of knowledge is the essence of virtue. It is the knowledge that assesses the claims of others in due relation to one's own. The failure to do so is virtue's opposite, vice. Vice is excess or defect, excess in the indulgence of one's passions, excess in encroachment on the rights of others, defect in the lapses of service and the negligences of responsibilities to others or to oneself.

Knowledge of this kind is harder to attain than most other kinds. It cannot be learned as we learn facts, items of information, or the routine techniques of the ordinary crafts or skills. All sorts of influences—prejudices, distractions, passions—resist its acquisition. The drive of the self for dominance breeds envies, jealousies, ambitions, fears that pervert our judgment and induce the excesses and defects that cloud self-knowledge.

Virtue is knowledge from another aspect as well. It is the courage of knowledge that makes us free. But knowledge, the knowledge that teaches truth, reaches to the bottom of a fathomless well, and all we obtain are glimpses and snatches. Nevertheless they are enough to direct our thoughts along lines that show the falsity of many of our prejudices. There is in the first place the scientific probe into the nature of the universe itself.

Science has been remarkably successful thus far in discovering the measurements of things, the ratios, proportions, equations, distances, speeds, combinations, pushes and pulls of things. But all this knowledge is still in an important sense only symbolic, symbolic of truth that goes far beyond our most penetrating insights. Nevertheless the advancement of science has brought not only a vast increase in our power to construct, to control, and to destory, not only the ability to raise living standards and to combat diseases, but also, if we open our minds to it, some liberation of our entire being. Such liberating knowledge, often blocked by our preconceptions, is slowly gained. One aspect of it is the knowledge of law, law that cannot be violated, evaded, or set aside by magic, prayer, or wishful thinking. We are compelled to recognize the inviolate nature of universal law, even if we still tend to keep it in one compartment of our minds, ignoring its application to others. Whenever we drive a car, or press an electric button, we are aware in whatever measure of the forces that inevitably control the operation. The wider ranges of this knowledge help to dispel our false concepts of nature. We no longer regard the thunderbolt as flung by Zeus or the blasting hail in summer as God's punishment for transgression. And if we still pray for rain, it is more as an outlet for our anxiety than as a sincere expression of the belief that God will listen and end the drought. We no longer believe that the night woods are haunted by spirits.

Thus we are liberated from false hopes and false fears. Perhaps we may miss the comfort that false hopes can bring. And some of us may miss the more pleasant creations with which the human imagination populated the woods and the mountains, the dryads and oreads and water nymphs and dancing fairies, but we can instead appreciate the real and more marvelous wonders of nature, if only we have enough of the same imagination that created these insubstantial phantoms. Besides, such playful fancies had less hold, less influence over the untutored mind, than the dark and sinister incarnations that foreboded death and disaster and sowed the seeds of pestilence and threatened men even after death with the ghostly murk or the everlasting misery of Hades, Gehenna, or Hell. Such superstitions clouded the outlook and stultified the imagination. The knowledge that liberates men from them must surely be counted a source of power.

One serious obstacle to the application of scientific knowledge within the area of our long-established beliefs is that our moral and spiritual values are embodied in them and have received their greatest expression in times when scientific knowledge was minimal. Consequently they are attached to conceptions of the universe that are highly erroneous. The values themselves are intrinsically independent of the cosmological framework in which they are incorporated, and some moderns save the ethics at the cost of the theology by treating the cosmic tales, the notions of Heaven and Hell and an anthropomorphic God, of the picturesque rewards and the awesome punishments He metes out, as myths or parables adapted to the comprehension of the peoples to which they were addressed.

The reconciliation of religion and science thus achieved has the advantage that it removes an otherwise serious obstacle to the acceptance of certain implications of scientific knowledge, but it is at best only partial. When the conception of God becomes amorphous, a name for the unknown presumptive creator of the universe, the sanctions of the old faith that depended on His revealed will are loosened. Human values are rooted in the social nature of man, and man himself is a rather significant revelation of the potentialities of nature itself. The philosophy of religion—theology, if you prefer—needs more positive underpinnings.

With apologies for these irrelevant comments we return to the role of the advancement of science. If we contemplate the already known scale of the universe, in which our planet is a small satellite of one sun in a galaxy of millions of suns, which in turn is but one in a vast system of galaxies tending over unreckonable billions of light-years, we can no longer conceive of the God presumed to be the maker of this stupendous universe as a jealous superhuman being who dictates a code of laws for the inhabitants of this cosmically insignificant earth—or for one little people in particular—and is waiting to reward or punish every single one of them according to his deserts. But we would enlarge our vision of the nature of things, appreciate the better its wonders and its magnificence, grateful that we are so made that we can be conscious of all this. We would then abate the false prides that betray us so that we vaunt the "master race," the "chosen people," the "Lord's anointed," and make other overweening claims that reject our common humanity, and we would rid ourselves of some of the witless false responsibilities we assume as curators of eternal destiny.

We are creatures of desire, so that we must forever pursue some goals. We seek endlessly the unattained, the never-to-be-fully-attained. To live is to want and to want is to value. Power is simply means to values. Our values are not the findings of science nor can science prove them true or false. But science can ratify or correct or destroy the framework of myth in which we incorporate our values, the beliefs that postulate the relation of our values to the great scheme of things. Many such beliefs are the creatures of our untutored imaginings, of our dreams and our hopes, of our needs and of our fears. On this basis the beliefs themselves grow and proliferate, become formalized and sanctified. The real danger begins when the creative process that initially produced them is arrested or atrophied by the taboos of orthodoxy. The vision of which they were the outcome is then obscured, and the myths harden into dogmas, preventing the development of more enlightened beliefs. From this danger new knowledge, scientific knowledge, can rescue us, restoring the freedom of the creative mind and thus endowing it with new power.

It was once a famous saying: "It is certain because it is impossible." Tertullian's saying has the ring of a robust mysticism, but it is perilous wherever it controverts clear scientific evidence. The paradox comes too close to the attitude of those who refuse to know lest it weaken their cherished beliefs or who keep their knowledge in one mental compartment and their faith in another. Our interests and our ambitions, our comfortable assurances, our hopes and even our fears combine with our credulities to give us distorted views of the actualities we must meet in our daily lives as well as of the greater realities that stretch far beyond our vision. We live in a society that seeks with a thousand discordant voices to convince and to cajole us with blandishments and promises and warnings and incitements, offering us wealth and security and peace of mind, cures for the ailments of the body or the "soul." The voices range from the utterance of the devotees of this or that great cause to the loose rhetoric of office seekers and the more raucous appeals of the patent-medicine promoter.

By their creeds men must live, by the meaningfulness of their value-laden visions, insights, or myths. Our religious creeds, however, mostly combine ethical or spiritual insights with outdated cosmologies, and people generally have not enough trust in the values enshrined in their creeds unless they are buttressed by the doctrines that modern science must reject. So they ignore or evade the knowledge they cannot reconcile with their orthodoxies. Demanding certainty, they gain only uncertainty by such evasions. There are many areas to which our knowledge does not reach, but for the areas to which it does penetrate it is weakness and escapism to refuse its enlightenment. So men grope in shadows of their own making, shunning the light beyond, and they fight in the shadows with shadowy enemies, vain battles over unreal issues and outmoded formulas, where "ignorant armies clash by night."

So far we have spoken of the knowledge of nature, of the world around us, suggesting how it might clarify our visions and recreate our creeds, the vehicles that embody our values. Such achievements, we must note in passing, will not be the automatic results of receptivity to our new knowledge of the universe but instead would come through the slow gestation and the travail that the birth of every important creation demands.

The signal advance attained in our knowledge of external nature is giving a strong spur to the lagging sciences of man himself, to the understanding of human nature, in ourselves, in others, in our relations to others, as revealed in the multifarious ways and dealings of groups and nations. This is a subject that will further engage us in later chapters. Here we shall limit ourselves to some comments on the relevance of this kind of knowledge to our social creeds.

We are commended to "see things steadily and see them whole." It is hard to see things steadily and practically impossible to see them whole. We must resort to shortcuts to express what we can grasp of the nature and significance of the greater realities, as well as for convenience of reference and economy of effort. The chief of these necessary shortcuts are symbolizations and typifications, symbols being images or concrete representations of intangible realities, and types being generic concepts denoting what is common to the members of inclusive systems. All our discourse is interlarded with symbols and type-characterizations. For example, we freely resort to symbols when referring to groups or nations. Uncle Sam is a popular symbol for the United States, and the Stars and Stripes a more official symbolization of it. The throne is a symbol of majesty, as the altar is of holiness and sacrifice. Examples of simple typifications are our common "isms," such as radicalism, republicanism, modernism, and so on.

Our ways of thought are channeled by our symbols and our typifications. Our work, our play, our planning, our living, our worshiping are all permeated with them. We pin down everything by assigning it to a type, and then we find a ready symbol for the type. But, necessary as these shortcuts are, they often enough prove a bar to the entry of new knowledge and have a skewing effect on the knowledge we already possess. We think we know what something is when we attach a symbol to it. We think we know what a person is when we assign him to a type—he is, say, a priest, a "red," a beatnik, or a highbrow. Our types and symbols become stereotypes, shibboleths, images surcharged with our emotions, passions, interests. They float and sway in a mist of ambient misconceptions.

Thus beguiled, we no longer strive to see people as they are. Instead we look on our images of them. It would seem to make little difference whether our contact with them is rare or frequent, near or remote. White Americans, for example, are liable to have a certain image of the Negro and another of, say, the Chinese. Most see the Chinese seldom and many see the Negro practically every day. The image is scarcely modified by experience, even when it is grotesquely distorted. It is particularly resistant to reality when our traditions are reinforced by our habituations. When, however, it is mainly our interests that are involved, the image is by no means so stubborn, since these depend on changing conditions. Under such conditions our images may undergo remarkable transformations, as has frequently happened, for example, in our relations with foreign powers. During World War II, we were wont to picture the Russians as sturdy, brave, inherently decent human beings. They were Communists then as they are today, and under a more brutal government than they have now, but after the war our relations deteriorated rapidly, and our image of the people themselves has grown less sympathetic.

Unfortunately for the course of history, our images of foreign peoples are always simplified, foreshortened by distance, and nearly always distorted for the worse. Since these images meet head on with the no doubt equally unflattering images they usually cherish of us, it is not surprising that gross misunderstandings complicate the intrinsic problems of relationship. It is so everywhere in the world of nations. Beyond any calculation is the wastage of human resources and lives—and the consequent setback to the creative forces within society—that have resulted from the misconceptions nations cherish of other nations, with the consequent underestimation of the other side that has so often made both sides confident of victory in the endless series of wars between them. For centuries, for example, the English and the French embroiled one another in ravaging wars, and what did it all avail to either side? The wastage of power through misunderstandings, misunderstandings due to egoistic prides and the false assumptions they generate, can be illustrated from every area of intergroup and international relationships.

Thus the unhappy plight of the Southern states of the Union, ranking lowest among the states in economic level, health conditions, and other indices of well-being, can reasonably be attributed to the manner in which they have dealt with the difficult problem posed by their large Negro populations. Nurtured on misconceptions, they have met the problem the wrong way, by the passionate refusal to permit the Negro to develop his capacities in decent cooperation with the whites. In a not too dissimilar way, the French refused to recognize the insurgent nationalistic demands of the Algerians and only after many years of enfeebling warfare did a French statesman show the courage and the wisdom needed to achieve the acceptance of the inevitable line of solution.

A more elusive type of misunderstanding is packed into the manner in which we employ our "isms" and other summary designations of principles or systems. It is natural, and laudable enough, that we should regard the systems in which we have been brought up as good, or at least better than opposing systems. But we tend to draw black-and-white distinctions between other people's systems and our own. And we unwisely assume that because our systems are good for us they must be good for other people as well. For example, we approve of democracy and hold that, say, the new nations of Africa ought forthwith to adopt it. We do not realize that it takes generations of preparation before a new and resourceless people can adopt a system that among ourselves has taken many generations to develop. Again, the average American regards capitalism as an eminently desirable system and Socialism as a thoroughly bad one. But he does so in a foggy way. Actually, the United States, like all modern industrial orders—with the exception of the Soviet extreme—is a socio-capitalist system. Its highways, its Federal Reserve Bank, its social-welfare legislation, its provision for veterans, its agriculture controls, its numerous regulatory commissions, its Tennessee Valley Authority, and numerous other governmental controls are all socialistic. The problem is primarily where the line should be drawn, what should remain in the private enterprise domain whether to safeguard our fundamental liberties or for greater efficiency; and different industrial democracies draw the line in different ways. But by regarding capitalism as an absolute and Socialism as an opposing absolute, we confuse the issues and take our fighting stand on insecure ground. This attitude, though now somewhat modified, has had unhappy consequences in blurring our anti-Communist propaganda and in alienating some of the new ex-colonial states which, since they have no private capital acquisitions, must resort to various socialistic programs for the development of their resources. Here as elsewhere, the failure of our understanding of the conditions, the failure to utilize knowledge lying at our hands, is also the weakness of our power.

The politician on every level of authority is peculiarly exposed to the temptation to ignore the knowledge he may possess, where it does not suit his designs or where it runs counter to popular prejudice, while at the same time the many immediate demands on his attention make it difficult for him to acquire the knowledge requisite for the decisions he must make. It is an old saying that the government of men is conducted with only a mite of intelligence. In the misgoverned Athens of the fourth century B.C., Plato concluded that men will not be governed aright "until philosophers are kings." To us it sounds like a ridiculous utterance from an ivory-tower oracle. But by "philosopher" Plato meant "lover of wisdom," which was the initial meaning of the term. And while the hurly-burly of politics and the endless rivalry for power may never permit the achievement of his goal, we can at a minimum hope the day has already come, in the light of the appalling power that science has supplied to government, when no great country can be so befuddled by passion or prejudice as to permit another Stalin or another Hitler or another Mussolini, under whatever guise, to rule over it.

9.

Personality as Power

All the manifestations of power that operate in human society are set in motion by the action either of an individual or of a group. In all instances personality is the final determinant, whether acting of its own accord or in the conjunctions and opposition of personalities within some organization. We shall therefore consider in succession the nature of personality as power and of organization as power.

All life is power-hungry, according to its kind, pursuing its objectives through the particular modes of power for which it is equipped. Life in this respect is motivated energy. Personality in this respect is the unified complex of motivations or drives inherent in the individual. The developed personality is the resultant of the modes the power quest has followed. This is equally so whether the personality is aspiring or meanspirited, robust or weak, intelligent or stupid, warmly sympathetic or narrowly self-centered. To seek anything is to exert power in order to achieve it. Even the most withdrawn, quiescent, or contemplative types want power, exert power, in order to assure the inner quietude that is by no means the easiest of objectives to obtain or to maintain. The changing pattern of the passing years, the incessant changes of one's environment and of one's relationships to others, the changes that every success and every failure bring, all call for the exercise of power.

All men seek power, in their respective ways and for their respective ends. We have noted the tendency to think of power as though it meant only the ruder or more external kinds of control—commanding obedience, commanding goods, disposing of resources, sanctioning activities, ruling over other men, enforcing one's will. Our argument here depends on the recognition that the philosopher in his study is employing power no less than the riveter on the job, that the great artist at his easel is no less a master of power than the great general in the field. Likewise, the tender blade of grass that lifts through the earth is exhibiting power no less than the earthquake—and who shall say that the former power is not at least as significant as the latter? Life has incredible secret powers that take whole ages to reveal. The highest manifestations up to the present time of this vital power are the expressions of human personality.

To indicate roughly the great diversity of ways in which personality exhibits itself let us take one aspect of its activity, the occupational, selecting a series of categories as they range from those most concerned with the external types of power to those that depend on development of the inner capacities of the mind or spirit. Our description must be limited to a few types and can deal only with their more characteristic features. We should also note that within each category there are members who are entirely aberrant from the type as described.

First, we take the professional soldier. Most men are soldiers because their country calls them to serve, not because they want to make military service their occupation. The professional soldier, like any other occupational category, appears in many different guises with many variant dispositions, but the typical professional soldier, the man who chooses military service as his career—and we should exclude here the various technical services, such as engineering, electronics, medicine, and so forth, that are common to both military and nonmilitary service—has certain rather well-defined characteristics. He tends to place high esteem on rank and status and on the meticulous etiquette of command. He loves the kind of order that is highly articulated and well-defined, whether it is the order he imposes on those below him or the order he obeys at the command of those above him. The cause for which he fights is always right. It must be so, as psychological assurance because he fights for it. On most issues he has very positive opinions; he does not concern himself with pros and cons. He is usually antidemocratic in feeling and conservative in policy. For him the troops he commands are units in a power system, trained to appear as uniformly alike as possible, and consequently he tends to see them not so much as individuals who have their own lives to live and their own values to cherish but as numbered items possessed of a common, very common, humanity.

At one extreme of the professional soldier range comes the militarist variety. He believes in settling differences by force, as the only conclusive method, though he is usually blind to the progeny of troubles that such a settlement, if indeed obtained, entails. He used to assert that warfare was salutary for the nation, purging the "softness" of the times of peace and evoking the highest qualities of which man is capable, invincible courage, supreme devotion, vindicating the natural law of the survival of the fittest, which of course is always the country to which he himself belongs. He is extrovert, narrowly forthright, much more interested in "manly" sports than in the finer arts. He may by quick-tempered or coolly calculating, bluff or sarcastic, but nearly always within the same limited range of vision.

Next in order we take the adventurer. Here we have many varieties. There is the speculator, who is out to make a fortune by clever scheming, by taking big risks, manipulating, juggling funds, floating companies, and so forth. He has a vision of the future, his future, based on an optimistic view of his own destiny and of his ability to surmount obstacles. Then there is a species of explorer who follows up untrodden trails, seeking the pride of being first, eager to write or help write the tale of how he did it. He may be, for example, a mountain climber, to whom an uncharted peak, or a ridge no one has traversed before, is a personal challenge. To conquer it first he is ready to face the perils of the most inclement, most insecure, most toilsome, and most painful of all the ways of travel. Or he may be another type of record-seeker, the athlete, or again the big-game hunter, who spends strenuous years of preparation to have his name recorded on a cup or on a framed specimen exhibited over the mantlepiece.

What is common to all the varieties of this type is that alike they throw themselves intensively into a risk-fraught endeavor to achieve a single easily identified once-for-all objective, which has no obvious relation to any lifetime pursuits. The speculator differs from the others in that his get-rich-quick objective gives him the means to obtain wealth and a certain amount of power, though it furnishes no preparation toward any intrinsic goal and may indeed be a detriment in that respect. The other kinds of adventurer can utilize their success to enter some occupation related directly or indirectly to the field of their endeavor while they bask in the glow of the kudos already won, but their climactic period is likely to be short and comes too early in life to ensure any future. Consequently there may develop various strains and a feeling of letdownness in the abrupt ending of the activity that had so totally absorbed them before.

We take next in order the entrepreneur. He is the established man of affairs whose great objective is expansion. He digs in, works hard and incessantly, seizes opportunities as they arise, and directs his actions and his thoughts to the prospects of development, "progress," the greater future. He enjoys the competitive struggle, keen-eyed for any advantage over his rivals; assiduously assessing the present, he lives for the future. He keeps his outside interests within strict bounds. Even when he goes home in the evening, he carries his problems and sometimes his actual work along with him. When he feels the need to unbend, he is not unlikely to resort to the occasional fling of some brief dissipation, but he rarely lets himself get entangled in such episodes in ways that would distract him from his business, the real business of life.

The entrepreneur is found everywhere over the whole broad area of affairs, and some of the members of the categories that follow might be included as possessing the characteristics of this type. It is characteristic of him that he is so obsessed with "progress" as he understands it that it becomes "progress" without a goal. To quote a Latin saying, "For the sake of living he loses the ends of living." The acquisition of means, in other words, becomes an end in itself, beyond which he scarcely looks. His power drive is outgoing, reaching out merely to the more. So the zest of life may center in the battle of wits, the lift he feels in the contest, and especially when he wins an edge over his competitors. The register of success is profit, and profit as it grows becomes prized more for the prestige and control it brings than for its purchasing power.

Our next major category is that of the professional. The term "profession" has broadened out in various directions, but we are thinking here primarily of certain longer-established professions, the doctor, lawyer, teacher, scientist, engineer, architect. Here we find several quite significant features that have not previously appeared. In the first place every genuine professional worker is concerned with his subject field for its own sake, for its own value, not merely and often not mainly for ulterior ends. The work has its intrinsic interest, and thousands of others are cooperating with him in advancing it. All of them are his colleagues, though some may be rivals and on occasion a few may be competitors. A man can excel in business, though his interest in it is primarily in the return. But no one can excel as a scholar or an architect or a scientist unless he finds a deep satisfaction in the quality of the work he does.

The majority of professionals are paid a stated salary or else receive fees according to some schedule from clients who solicit their services. Consequently the competitive element within a profession is less direct and usually much less intense than in the business arena. The fee-receiving professional, the doctor or engineer or lawyer, may become a more or less routine practitioner, but for real achievement in his profession he must love his work and keep in touch with developments in his field. Back of that he must have the consciousness that the art he practices is based on a science that is always growing and has unexplored reaches without end. The skilled craftsman has in degree the same responsibility—for real achievement he must seek and find satisfaction, a measure of fulfillment, in the quality, beauty, finish of his work.

For the professional practitioner, somewhat in contrast with the businessman, there is liable to arise an ambivalence of conflict of objectives. The businessman is more likely at times to have a conflict between his ethics and his competitive interest. The financial advantage of the practitioner may be at odds more directly with his professional service. The lawyer has some special problems of this kind. We shall take, however, the case of the doctor. The profession, properly enough, is anxious to maintain full control over the manner in which its services are rendered, and it has established a stricter code than any other profession upholds. This concern, however, is a power interest as well as a service interest, and the power interest on occasion may combine with an economic interest to promote a bias, no doubt often an unconscious bias, against measures that may be in the public interest but would diminish the full autonomy of the profession. Organized medicine has been almost invariably opposed to governmental measures providing state-organized medical insurance or free medical service to the needy who without public subvention are unable to obtain adequate treatment. In our next chapter we shall have to consider a not dissimilar type of problem that affects the public official, whether as executive or as politician.

We end our brief list with the artist, and, among many contenders for the qualification, we include primarily the composer, the poet, the painter, the author, the sculptor, the interpretative musician, the actor. Some members of our professional category belong here as well, when their work exhibits inventive originality, fine intuition, creativeness of some kind—the architect, for example, the moviemaker, the designer, the couturier, the interior decorator, the furniture maker, the potter, the cartoonist. Artistry in some degree is an attribute inhering in all work of high quality. Artistry is creative expression, the revelation through whatever medium of significant form in a manner that confers on it a distinctive individuality. Art is the purest and fullest revelation of personality as power.

Art is a special kind of creation. The scientist and the technologist are also creators, bringers of something new to men. Science reveals the hitherto unknown, and technology produces constructs and devices that are more efficient than any that existed before. What the artist does, however, is something else than add a stone or, as the greatest scientists do, a whole compartment to the ever-increasing edifice of knowledge, something else than devise apparatus of greater efficiency than any that existed before. The work of the greatest scientific genius is supplemented and further advanced and modified by his successors. The new apparatus is rather quickly outmoded by later developments. What the artist achieves, the great artist, remains new and unsurpassed. Succeeding artists do not improve on it, do not advance beyond it. Nobody improves on the work of a Homer or Praxiteles or Dante or Shakespeare or Rembrandt or Goethe, or for that matter on the work of a Racine or Dryden or Dickens or Proust or Whitman or Shaw or of a great many others across the wide range of the arts, whether in Europe or in the Orient or over the Americas. The once-happy conjuncture of personality and situation can never be repeated. What these artists have achieved endures and continues to touch the thoughts and the hearts of men, in smaller or larger circles of influences as the years go by.

The integral power of the artist consists in the liberated communication of his unique personality. Communication in any one of many media is capable of endless variety, endless modulation, so that the gifted spirit can convey to the whole receptive world, the most intimate, the most delicate, the most profound thoughts. This art is thus, alone of all human achievements, potentially immortal. In this respect the founders of the great religions must be regarded as supreme artists.

We have sought to trace in broad lines some modes in which the drive of personality as power is executed in the functioning occupational categories. We have not tried to classify personality types themselves——there are too many ways of doing so where individual differences are endless and subtly distinctive. The interactive and counteractive impact of these incalculable differences of personality creates and sustains the cultural quality, indeed the very texture of a society. In our first contacts with others we tend to see them as types, but the more we come to know them we discover how inadequate and how often misleading our relegation of them to this or that type was. Our relations with them are at first simple, but they grow more complex and more significant when relationships continue and develop. Our enjoyments and our griefs, our successes and our failures, our idle gossiping and our serious discussion, our understanding of ourselves as well as of others depend at every stage on the impact on us of other personalities, as they attract or repel us, as they serve us or we serve them, as we are responsive or irresponsive to them.

The great leaders redirect the forms and forces of society, affecting the daily lives of large numbers. Their policies are determined by the way they interpret situations, but it is never merely a matter of cold reasoning; it is always the outlook of a particular personality that distinguishes these policies. Winston Churchill, for example, faced the dire needs of England in her time of greatest peril in a manner that was wholly characteristic of his own personality. Across the Channel, De Gaulle represented France in a manner that was peculiarly characteristic of himself, of his sense of France's greatness and of his own proud spirit, with its virtues and its foibles. Even more directly, the great artists and thinkers impress their personalities on their society, changing the tenor of men's ideas in the process of the generations.

The particular series of occupational categories we selected roughly follows a certain order, in accordance with the modes of power they mainly represent, and correspondingly, though with many variations and exceptions, of the types of personality most likely to be directed to them. Thus we passed from the occupational category that requires massive display of material force and calls for a rather rigid order of command and subordination to one that depends on the free creativity of the untrammeled individual.

The interest associated with function or occupation is, however, by no means the only concern that determines the manner in which the occupational task is performed. The advancement of the functional objective may be crossed by or even subordinated to other objectives not relevant to the task in hand. The drive for other forms of power finds expression in the office of the executive, in the workshop, in the council chamber. These other objectives cooperate at times with the functional objective, at others, and quite frequently, they compete with it, distort it, or betray it. Especially in the earlier stages of attainment they are rather likely to cooperate. Ambition spurs the youth to work devotedly and give his best to his task in order to win some much coveted recognition. The urge to be important, to make his way to the top, spurs the entrepreneur, in the full flush of his energy, to incessant driving work, to the full exercise of his ingenuity, regardless of other concerns. The captain works to win his spurs, to gain the notice of his superiors, not only for the sake of the cause or the country, but because of the distinction or honor it may bring him. The astronaut disciplines himself endlessly for the perilous exploration of space, and the duty he feels to the service is rein-

forced by the hope that success will bring him the further reward
of high acclaim.

But the identification of self-interest with occupational function is only partial, and the sense of responsibility to the functional
collectivity is frequently enough overborne by the urgency of other
drives. The eagerness for distinction, for personal advantage of
some kind, for greater popularity and the enhanced power it
brings may prove curiously out of accord with the adequate fulfillment of function. The public is taken by appearances and is
usually a poor judge of intrinsic merit. To court popularity, to
obtain the verdict of the public, to gain the reputation of being
successful, one may betray his responsibility. The professional practitioner is subject to this temptation. The lawyer, eager to win his
case, is tempted to resort to dubiously legal or to unethical devices
for this end. The ambition of the prosecuting attorney may per-
suade him to the more serious offense of suppressing or distorting
relevant evidence in order to secure a conviction. The doctor on
occasion is tempted to cater to the wishes of his patient, where
they are ill-advised and unconducive to health. In every profession
situations occur in which financial interest or the prospect of advancement or the opportunity for public recognition is at odds
with the requirements of professional integrity. The intrinsic satisfactions of accomplishment are beset by temptations to sacrifice
them in favor of extrinsic rewards, emoluments, positional advantages, the power to influence people; and conscience may not
be strong enough to hold the balance aright.

This competition of interests is a particularly insidious danger
for the artist. Creative work, seen in its freest and purest form in
the realm of the fine arts, is peculiarly demanding, since it requires
not only devotion but also an utter sincerity in the devotion. Creation is always travail. What the artist is endeavoring to do is to

express something new and different, something never before expressed as he wants to express it. He must do so through some common medium of expression, language or paint on canvas or stone or wood or metal. The medium resists his efforts to convey the full import of his thoughts or feelings. What makes it the harder is that the artist himself is groping for a clearer grasp of what he feels or thinks and cannot make that fully manifest except as he successfully wrestles with the difficulties of his medium.

On every level of creative work, the major problem of the artist is the same—to maintain unflinching sincerity while striving to express his vision, to make the medium convey as nearly as possible the full import of his design. If he succeeds in gaining recognition, he has now the additional temptation to supply his public with some replica of his first success, becoming his own copyist and thereby losing the integrity of his first devotion. This temptation increases as the artist grows older and inertia gains on him. The truly great artist is too deeply committed to his task to be deflected by mere vainglory, but the lesser artist is liable to yield, catering to his public or keeping in line with the artistic vogue, blunting the edge of his communication in order to widen its range. So the novelist who has made a hit or the painter whose exhibit has been hailed by the critics is in danger of pursuing his past success instead of spurring on his inventive power to fresh efforts. Creation is a precarious as well as an arduous business. When invention flags, one seeks the more eagerly the extraneous reward, the ribbon and the laurel—and the purse.

We have left to the last the occupational area where the conditions are most formidably arrayed against integrity of purpose, that of the politician. He lives in an atmosphere of compromise, and the distinction between the compromise that is necessary to assure as far as is feasible the success of the measures in which he genuinely believes and the compromise that is best calculated to keep him in power is easily obscured. The politician has to please a many-voiced following both to hold his position and to have any influence in the making of policy. He has to make promises he knows he may be unable to keep. He lives in a world of oppositions. He has constantly to attack in order to defend. There are always those who are eager to oust him and take his place. His own interest and the pressures of his party urge him to give his public what they want to hear, whether he believes it or not, whether it is in accordance with the facts or not. He must be persuasive at all costs. The public are impressed by appearances and they want their prejudices fed. He is tempted to make secret deals with the influential people who can throw their weight on his side. It is unlikely he would be in politics at all if he didn't have a strong urge for power, and for the perquisites of office.

Politics, says a modern writer, is always a choice of the second-best—or nearly always, not only for the politician himself but also for those who vote for him. Expediency weighs more than principle. Only the greater statesman, in his greater moments, can take an unswerving stand without evasions or concessions, trusting to his convictions and prepared to put them to the test. To this conclusion we must add, however, that the politician's sense of responsibility is in great measure a reflection of the moral temper of his times and of the alertness and political education of the electorate.

One of the greatest dramas of human life is the manner in which the intrinsic aspiration of the human mind or spirit, the sense of the responsibility to develop one's potentialities, to achieve and to create, is beset by the drag of conditions, by more immediate urgencies, by the appetite for material gains and the more material power they offer. Frequently these conspiring forces win

out against the earlier promise. Balking circumstances, disillusion-
ments, the weariness of unrewarded endeavor, habits of indulgence, the growing desire for ease, and the diminution of energy
turn the once-aspiring mind from the unyielded satisfactions and
the arduous toils of achievement to the extraneous gratifications
of position, rank, money, and power over other men. It is the
politician who fails otherwise to make good who is most likely to
become a demagogue or a local boss. The ambitious labor leader
who cannot succeed on the strength of his achievements and his
personality is the kind who is the most likely to tie in with corrupt
politicians or with gangsters. The author who fails to find a market may gain a niche by resorting to sensationalism or lubricity.

Life is a ceaseless exercise of power to effect changes for its
own accommodation, change within as well as without. For human beings, once the minimal conditions necessary to sustain life
have been secured, the direction of change comes under the guidance of personality. The leader, the prophet, the schemer, the adventurer, the inventor are constantly at work promoting the ways
of change, eroding resistances, modifying the established culture.
The vision of the new is supported by the discontents of the old.
The supporters of the old at length lose ground, and the diagonal
of change advances amid the strife of loyalties. Somehow, out of
it all, there emerges the new climate of the times, the subtly moving culture of the age. In the great melee, many are devotees of
material power, the control of means, the control of men. These
are the captains and the kings, the men of the iron fist, the rough-
riders, the autocrats, the bureaucrats parading their proud brief
authority. But always there are the inner-directed seekers after
significance, new knowledge, new interpretations, new understandings, significance of content or significance of form and tex-

ture, ranging through all the finer arts and skills, the sciences and the philosophies. And it is these, the men who most impress their personality on their work, who in the longer run are the prime engineers of society.

10.

Organization as Power

The first organization, the family, was geared to shelter, protect, order, and sustain its members. The enlarged family, the kin, fulfilled the same functions on a wider scale. Organization existed where society existed, wherever man existed. Organization is the most elementary as well as the most advanced source and form of power, power as means to every human end.

But from the beginning and right through to the present, organization has been at once a means of power and a limit of power. The bond of union was also the barrier of union. When the kin became the bond of union, it meant that kin were set against kin. Neighboring kins or tribes were alien to one another, and alien meant dangerous, to be defended against, on occasion to be attacked. Natural man, in primitive times and often enough now, tends to think in absolutes, in sharp dichotomies. He that is not with us is against us. What is ours is good, what is theirs is suspect, and most likely evil. The clan allegiance, the tribal spirit—extolled, promoted, and strongly demarcated by festivals and celebrations and by the interest of the headmen—was the guarantor of security and also the ground of insecurity. It took ages before men perforce learned that loyalty to their tribe need not rule out the formation of a more inclusive union, that of the country, the people of many tribes, the nation. Today we have some new countries struggling to achieve this union, states created before their time, or states aborning, still sundered by tribal resistances. Such is the situation in certain areas of Africa, in the Congo, for example, and in Kenya.

We tend to think of the destitution in which the vast majority of mankind have lived up to our own times as essentially due to the lack of the techniques, mechanisms, and sources of power that have so greatly increased the productivity of labor in our industrialized countries. But across the known history of mankind, the extreme poverty in which most peoples have lived has had another cause besides the niggardness of the soil they had not learned to cultivate well, besides the droughts and storms and plagues and diseases of crops or animals that beset them. Man could have attained over much of the earth some degree of humble comfort and would have had much better opportunities to develop his ingenuity for the improvement of his lot had it not been for the endless raids and invasions, increasing in devastating efficiency as better weapons of destruction were devised, resulting in ravaged towns and scorched earth and the destruction of forests that never grew again. One rather curious illustration of how the resources of poverty-stricken areas were squandered in the enmities of adjacent localities can still be seen in the prong of the Peloponnesus called the Mani. There in earlier times each village or little town defended itself against its neighbors by erecting high stone towers from which to throw down missiles at an advancing enemy, so that the whole area was dotted with these constructions, constantly renewed or heightened. So it went on through an age of wastage and tensions, with nothing in the end to compensate for it.

The logical principle of organization is that common interest is best safeguarded by coextensive common organization, limited so far as feasible to the range of the common interest itself and to the means necessary for its protection. In our day as never before, the most universal of all human interests is protection against the annihilating effects of modern warfare. The same forces that refused to expand the protection of common interest beyond the limits of the tribe, the limits of the city state, the limits of the petty principalities of the Middle Ages, now resist the organization of security beyond the limits of the nation or at best of some group of nations united only in their opposition to some other group of nations, thereby safeguarding only insecurity. The claims of sovereign powers and the interests that cluster around them defeat the peremptory logic of organization.

The problem of the inadequate state highlights another major principle of organization. By failing thus to provide security, the state is subordinating its major and age-old function of establishing law and order in favor of secondary or entirely extraneous considerations. An organization is set up to serve the more effectively certain interests of its members. Most voluntary organizations have one major interest, of greater or less amplitude. The state has the most inclusive of interests, the public welfare. But even this interest, as maintained by the state, is by no means all-inclusive, though modern dictatorships sometimes claim it to be. The limits of state control are usually set out in a constitution, but the state is also limited, directly or indirectly, by the majority opinion and by the limitations of its chief instrument, the law. In every case an organization exists in order to fulfill assigned functions. In this respect an organization is wholly different from a person, since the latter has a claim to exist in his own right and has values or ends that are not merely means to other values or ends, in other words, not merely functional or instrumental. Instead, the organization properly exists to serve not its own ends, but the ends of the persons who compose it or who control it. We speak of the "personality" of the organization, especially in its corporate form. But here the term signifies only the possession of certain legal rights to act for or on behalf of persons, and certain consequent liabilities or responsibilities. It does not mean that an organization has values of its own. The organization is an agency, a means, a system sustained by its members for their service. Its virtue, its sole virtue, is the service it renders.

The organization exists because it can do for its members things they cannot do for themselves or cannot do so well, or else because it can render service to a wider public they cannot provide, or provide as well, for themselves. An insurance system exemplifies the former type of service, a hospital is an example of the latter. Some voluntary organizations have a double purpose, for they both render service and make a profit from the service. The effects of this potential conflict of interests are less critical for business organizations, established primarily for profits, than for social welfare organizations, such as hospitals, houses for the aged, private schools, foster homes. The main ground for this conclusion is that private business concerns, supplying commodities and services to a general public, are nearly always in a competitive position and the consumer can show by his patronage his estimate of comparative values, imperfect as this estimate often is. The hospital and other such organizations are not seriously subject to this kind of check, nor even if it existed is the "consumer" qualified to assess the service.

Because of conflicts of interest, of one type or another, no organization whatever fulfills its service as well or as completely as it is technically capable of doing. Before we discuss what may seem to be an extreme statement, let us briefly consider in what respects an organization renders service beyond the capacity of individuals acting on their own or in a loose cooperative fashion. The power of organization is not to be understood as equivalent to the massed power of its members. It is not to be understood on the simple old analogy of the sticks that can be easily broken one by one but when bound tightly together have a vastly greater resistance. In union is strength but it is not merely the multiplication of unit strengths. An organization has its own specialized institutions, its own equipment, its own processes, its own modes of action. It possesses not only powers but also rights and privileges that private individuals never own and that are exercised only by its officials. It can command services not available to mere individuals. It has departments and experts specially geared to special operations. The manifold powers exercised by governments constitute the greatest example of purely organizational attributes, but every corporation exercises controls, conducts distinctive activities, and achieves distinctive results according to its kind.

Everywhere within this network of organization, with its graded positions and powers, its hierarchies and enclaves, there is room for the conflicts of interest that limit and skew the fulfillment of function. Officials, being human beings, are apt to use their powers and opportunities to serve their personal or group interests. They like to promote their friends, to give favor to those who can favor them in turn, to advance those underlings, regardless of comparative quality, who are most subservient or congenial to them. In some types of organization the same motives may lead to specious appeals to the membership at large, especially in times when the reelection of officials is at stake. In pursuing their interests, jealousies, envies, and suspicions are likely to develop within the staff, erecting further impediments to efficient, smooth operation. Finally there is the spur of financial advantage, the inducement for the official to feather his own nest, for executives to award themselves high salaries and stock options and other perquisities beyond reasonable claims for service. And when we turn to the categories of workers they, too, especially when their unions are powerful, can find ways of adding needless costs, through devices for slowing down operations, featherbedding, and so forth.

In the previous chapter we commented on certain conflicts of interest that may interfere with the efficiency of the individual's discharge of his responsibility, apart from his organizational commitments. Such conflicts increase in number, in intensity, and in complexity when the individual becomes an executive or a representative of an organization of any scale.

Official power is power held in trust for the service of an agency. But what, besides the integrity of the official, assures the fulfillment of this trust? Power is skilled in guarding itself against its guardians. The procedures of corporate bodies are conducted in private and sometimes undisclosed in their records. The public know little enough about the policies of governmental bodies which are presumed to be their agents or servants, or about the situations that may explain and possibly justify these policies. Opposition parties are less concerned to give the facts about them than to present interpretations favorable to themselves. The few clear well-informed exponents are stray voices lost in the uproar of propagandism. The greater the organization, the less are its plans and policies exposed to the rank and file. Moreover, there is so much compartmentalization, so much differentialization of authority, that all down the line schemes may be concocted and commissions from above handled in devious ways so that the busy schemers on top are never made aware of them. The reports sent to headquarters can be colored to suit the occasion. There are numerous ways in which the less scrupulous official can conceal or camouflage his less justifiable actions. Inspectors and examiners may be induced to refrain from exposing such actions or may be afraid of reprisals.

Business organizations have simple tests of efficiency that other forms, such as welfare organizations or political organizations, lack. A decline in profits, the failure of any section to keep up with others according to standards set, the inability of a firm to compete successfully with others of its own kind, such inefficiencies cannot long be concealed or explained away. The chief danger of continued inefficiency lies usually with the top management, which may manipulate finances to serve its private ends or fail to keep abreast with current developments in the industry or take an unduly speculative position or an unduly "conservative" one. Another danger, to which all types of organization are subject, is the tendency to autocracy that the possession of power stimulates in some high executives—general managers, presidents, chairmen of boards, or whatever they may be—especially as the length of tenure grows. Then they are prone to make decisions that properly fall to the more expert subordinates directly concerned and to overrule the recommendations of able men who have given special study to the problem at issue. And sometimes the top executive becomes jealous of the second-in-command, fearing the latter may be appointed his successor, and undermines his authority, without regard for the confusion and loss of initiative entailed.

Every organization strives to stake out an area in which it is dominant, or at the least important. It likes to establish a tradition of its own, on a smaller or a longer scale, and in this endeavor it is greatly aided by its potential immortality. It may formulate policies that long survive the formulators. It can plan for a long-term future. The organizational reach into the future enhances its present power and the importance of its leaders. It acquires its own characteristic usages, its own traditions, its own rituals. In the corporate form its holds it funds in perpetuity. Only a total and irremediable failure can kill it. Not infrequently, however, a corporation loses its separate identity by becoming merged in some larger one. There are also some organizations that by their very nature are dated, organizations set up for a temporary once-for-all objective, as, for example, those that a generation or two ago were established to help achieve women suffrage where it has now become the law of the land. But even they have been so tenacious of life that not infrequently they refused to die when their mission was accomplished, finding some follow-up reason for continued existence. The only type of organization that is indubitably mortal is the kind whose mortality is tied to mortality of its present members, say the veterans of a particular war or the survivors of some great disaster or again a group of persons who join together to memorialize some dated experience they have all shared.

The chief executives of any important organization tend to regard themselves as heirs to its undying authority, and as such they jealously guard it against encroachments. In consequence the organization and its institutions become for them values-in-themselves, not merely for the service they render. Lower down the line the officeholder is tempted to magnify his position and his value. This is the attitude to which the term "bureaucracy" is commonly applied. The bureaucrat in this sense is more concerned with the form of his service than with its utility. The convenience, comfort, and advantage of those served are subordinate to the sanctity of usage, to the requirements of red tape. This stricture is much less applicable to business organizations, which obviously cannot afford to offend the customer. Bureaucracy of this type has been notoriously prevalent in political offices. It has been the subject of much satiric comment, including the famous lines of Shakespeare, depicting the overbearing official who

> Drest in a little brief authority, . . .
> Plays such fantastic tricks before high heaven
> As make the angels weep.

No doubt a modicum of bureaucracy is called for as an assurance of order in the complex operation of a large-scale organization, but it easily becomes exaggerated into an enemy of efficiency. The typical bureaucrat is officious, jealous of his authority, the sedulous guardian of routine. Everything must go "through channels," passing through the hands of various intermediaries before it reaches the designated agent. Formal and verbose reports grow apace, with many duplicates of each to occupy stenographers and the filing clerks. "Parkinson's law," to the effect that the larger the staff the more work they create for themselves and for all the others, has too much validity to be dismissed as merely a caricature.

A swollen bureaucracy may be regarded as one of the diseases of organization. The incorporated "body," besides being designated in law a "persona" or a "corpus," is also rather frequently ——though very dubiously—spoken of as an organism. In one respect it certainly resembles an organism, being subject to ailments of its own. Its troubles are both complex and numerous. It has been the writer's lot to have carried out a series of investigations in the organizational field, and one or two examples from this experience may perhaps serve as illustrations, since the study of the subject is not yet far enough advanced to enable us to classify the various ailments.

Before doing so, let us remark that organizational health is a matter of degree. There are relatively healthy organizations and there are others that suffer from more or less serious ailments. The health of an organization consists in its efficacy to fulfill its designated functions, without wasteful internal friction or maladjustments and without the diversion of its powers or resources to irrelevant or ulterior ends.

To avoid any imputation on present managements, we shall take two cases dating back a considerable number of years. The first is that of an association set up by an important group of Protestant Church leaders not long after the First World War. They expressed much concern over the failure of the Christian churches to prevent the catastrophe of the war or mitigate its horrors. It was called The Inquiry into the Christian Way of Life and it was subsidized by a large foundation. Its objective was to explore ways in which professing Christians might be alerted to their obligation to promote peace on earth in accordance with the teachings of the Gospel. After a few years the director of the study, catering to the interest of some members of his staff and perhaps finding the mission too comprehensive or too undefined, quietly dropped the latter and crucial part of the title, so that it became known simply as The Inquiry. It directed itself to studies based on the theory that the members of a diversified group can reach a common viewpoint if discussion is conducted in the right spirit, to studies concerning prejudice, and to devices for the harmonious conduct of conferences. Some of the original founders began to express dissatisfaction. There were questions about the orientation of the staff and about the effectiveness of its work. The supporting foundation wanted evidence to justify, or otherwise, further subventions. The writer was invited to investigate the work being done and make a recommendation concerning its further financial support. After a period of investigation he concluded that the organization had lost its impetus, was not making any contribution sufficiently serious to justify prolonged financial support, but should be given one more year to enable its staff to conclude work in hand and to satisfy commitments made in their behalf. There was considerable protest from the leadership, which convoked meetings to denounce the report and reassert the value of the service. Nevertheless the course recommended in the report was carried into effect.

The second case we cite was that of a group of six Jewish agencies which had the common objective of combating discrimination and prejudice directed against Jews and other minority groups. While most of these organizations had in addition particular stated objectives of their own, the major emphasis was on this common objective and the funds they received from various sources, especially local Jewish communities, were largely contributed on that account. These agencies had grown in number and in scale in reaction to the monstrous genocide of the Hitler regime. They were generally known as defense agencies or community relations agencies.

As they expanded in size and in budget, a considerable volume of complaint developed on the part of their financial supporters, on the ground that the activities of the various agencies overlapped or duplicated one another, that they kept too much apart from one another where teamwork would be more effective and less wasteful of resources. The amount of budget funds they received, adding up to millions of dollars, was alleged to be disproportionate to any results they achieved. In fact it was impossible to prove to what extent, if any, they had been responsible for any significant improvement in the treatment of minority groups. To meet these objections an overall agency was created, an advisory council to "coordinate" their activities. The new agency, however, was merely advisory, and even so half of its voting power was in the hands of the operating agencies themselves. The result was that little was achieved in the way of coordination. The complaints kept on, and while some reports were made on the questions at issue they were discounted as coming from Jewish investigators who belonged to one or another of the many sections into which the Jewish community was divided. At length it was decided, though by no means unanimously, to invite an outside social scientist to study and report on the situation. The present writer, perhaps rashly, undertook the commission. His report was in several respects critical, and in particular presented adequate evidence of needless duplication and a lack of teamwork and of intercommunication. It proposed a system whereby certain duplicatory programs would be conducted through a single agency, distributing such assignments on what seemed a reasonable basis, the other agencies being requested to cooperate with the agency carrying the assignment. Various other changes were proposed, including the simplification of the top-heavy and highly expensive network of relationships the various agencies had separately established with Jewish centers throughout the country. The existing advisory council was to be strengthened and given fuller authority to review agency activities.

The report evoked a storm of controversy, a discordant combination of denunciation and approval. The upshot was that the two largest agencies broke away from the reconstructed advisory council, while the remaining four accepted the major recommendations and have since then joined forces more effectively than before.

The two cases above cited belonged broadly to the same area of the wide-ranging organizational spectrum, but they may serve to suggest the complex ways in which the objectives entrusted to organizations and the facilities they possess to implement them may be crossed, modified, or skewed by the personal and social interests of their leadership and staffs and not least by the motivations inherent in the possession of power. Every agency resolves itself into a network of human relationships. The vast growth of organizations has changed and continues to change the face of society, not only because it revolutionizes the workaday life of men but also because it throws them into multiple new contacts with their fellows, so that every organization becomes a seething center within which all human impulses find new expression.

The direct achievements of modern organization, with the elaborate equipment, mechanism, and energy potential of an ever-advancing technology—resources that only large-scale organization can develop and utilize—are always before our eyes, but we are less conscious of its indirect effects, its impact on the structure and character of society. In the first place it has been the greatest agent in the undermining of age-old social systems. As industrialism developed, the new massing of workers in factories and offices was initially the condition under which the owners and managers, men of the middle class, were able to amass capital and thus acquire power that overthrew the prerogatives of the hitherto ruling class, while at a later stage it provided the opportunity for the workers themselves to organize, creating trade unions enabling them to rise from exploitation to a considerable degree of dominance. In doing so they developed a new and highly effective form of power, the power that lies in the concerted withdrawal of service, the power that can stop the wheels of industry. Like every other form of power, this modern form has exhibited its dangers and its abuses, no less than its achievements.

It is obvious that the proliferation of massive and competing organizations, the power systems of the modern world, has not only changed the habits, attitudes, and expectancies of men but has created a whole series of new problems related to the order, security, and direction of society. There are problems of monopolistic bigness, of the manipulations and abuses of trust, of the clashes between organizational giants, of the personal freedoms of individuals caught in the meshes of corporate mechanism, of the control of government over entrenched private interests on which it must in important respects depend.

So we come to the final question. Bigness not only spells power but also tends to exalt the kind of power that expresses itself more in dominance and expansion than in the quieter processes of creative activity. What assurance can we find against such domination? Against usurpations of power, against the public injury that results from unresolved tests of strength between clashing organizations, between, say, intransigent unions and unyielding corporations? The only recourse we have lies in government. But here government cannot act as merely compulsive power. Such action would in various situations be politically inexpedient and socially impracticable. Its main reliance must be on the weight of its authority, on the one hand on its right to take any measures needed to sustain the public welfare, constituting it the final court of appeal for the settlement of all disputes that may endanger this welfare, and on the other hand on the recognition of that right by the citizens themselves. Without this recognition, authority is flouted, and the power of government becomes disruptive.

11.

The Transformations
of Power

We return to our distinctions between the various kinds
of power, as a preliminary to reviewing certain very significant
historical processes that have considerably reduced the relative role
and range of action of the most elementary of these forms. A
comment may first be made concerning the distinctions themselves.

The power that is displayed in all the motions of the physical
universe we speak of as energy, energy in its many manifestations
as light and heat, as X rays and gamma rays, as microwaves and
macrowaves of many descriptions. This primary energy, in its
equivalence with matter, is the very stuff of physical being. But
when we think of power in the realm of conscious being, entirely
new considerations come into play. Holding to the broad definition of power as the capacity to do things, to act, to effect change,
we must admit many kinds, many operations of power that are

wholly unknown to the purely physical nonconscious world. So
we can speak, for example, of the power of leadership, the power
of personality, the power of knowledge, the power of status or of
wealth, and so forth.

All these other powers, however, require a substratum of physical power. Without physical power, some modicum of energy,
nothing can be done. But by physical power alone, no human end
can be achieved, no conscious desire gratified. The wild beast
cannot pounce upon his prey without the perception of his senses,
without the guidance of his mite of intelligence. The power of
man to achieve his ends has been the product of the combination
of knowledge with energy, and the energy he employs has itself
been multiplied a millionfold by his increasing knowledge. This,
however, is but one aspect of the remarkable story of man's ever-
changing utilization of power.

Every rising civilization has been characterized by new developments in the control and application of power. One major direction has been the discovery of new techniques for the more
effective utilization of available power, while a more significant
development of later times has been the harnessing of new sources
of energy to do the work formerly performed, if performed at all,
by human toil or by domesticated animals. This is the great area
of technology, responsive to scientific advances. Another major
direction has been the limitations of physical enforcement, of
direct coercion, in the interrelations of groups and localities, for
the settlement of disputes, for the determination of authority, and
so forth. Other modes of control have very gradually become
operative over greater regions of society, as the scale of community
has been enlarged. This is the area of political government, a third
direction. Associated with and indirectly dependent on the first
two has been the enhancement and elevation of forms of power

that are remote from the need of physical reinforcement, the powers that find expression in the arts, the philosophies, the moral and spiritual movements of each passing age. The last of these directions, however, proceeds uncertainly back and forth, its changes exhibiting no clear trends, except possibly over whole epochs, unlike the second, which has reasonably clear stages of advancement, and wholly unlike the first, which, except when interrupted by cataclysmic disturbances, steadily advances from period to period and even, in our own time, from year to year.

It is easy to see how and why technological advance is a relatively steady progression. It was slowest under the conditions of primitive society, but each achievement has been the sure basis of further achievement, bringing to birth at particular junctures a greater discovery that was pregnant of a new era of technological development. Our own time is notably such a period. In the earliest human societies of record, man depended almost entirely on his own muscular power, digging roots, chasing animals, clubbing or spearing fish, building shelters by piling stones, making wattles with mud, laying a thatch of straw or reeds, and so forth. In the lack of better know-how, he had to depend for his sustenance, his home, his defense against enemies or wild beasts on the rude tools his own hands made. He had little recourse against storm or flood or drought and practically none against disease or pestilence. Gradually he learned to tame wild animals and use their energy for carrying or hauling, to collect seeds and scrape the soil in which they might grow. He discovered the wheel and its many uses. The early civilizations developed various devices, calculating systems, and simple mechanisms, advanced the decorative arts, and learned to erect more imposing structures, temples and palaces and the memorial tombs of the great. Technology advanced in various directions in the civilizations of the Orient and of the nearer

East, taken over and utilized in still more remarkable ways by the peoples of the Aegean, Crete, and Greece, and the Eastern Mediterranean, their contributions penetrating to Rome and through Rome to Western Europe. At length the West repaid its debt magnificently by inaugurating the more scientific study of nature, and thus came the great discoveries and practical inventions that in the eighteenth, nineteenth, and twentieth centuries placed at man's disposal vastly greater sources of energy than he had ever dreamed of before. In consequence the combination of poverty and drudge labor that had hitherto been the lot of all mankind except for small elites has become obsolescent and in the most advanced countries could already be wholly abolished by further improvements of the economy.

It is, however, another transformation of power, by no means unrelated to the first, that is our main concern in this chapter, a transformation that is assuming a climactic quality at the present time. It is a transformation in which the role of physical force in the ordering of social relationships has been significantly limited in its range as well as changed in its character. To clarify the complicated story, we shall distinguish some major stages of this transformation.

The first of these stages was signalized by *the establishment of the supertribal community,* the expansion of society beyond the confines of the blood bond, the enlarged family grouping. We have already commented on the significance of this development, but some further observations should be made in the present context. From the beginning, so to speak, human beings lived in familial clusters. The prolonged dependence of offspring on parents which differentiated human beings from the lower animals necessitated the family union, the first society, and the family became for social ends the greater family, the kin group. The associated kindred claimed its own exclusive living space, its locality, its area of sustenance. The limit of society was thus the tribe, the presumptive area of the blood bond. Within it developed the law of the tribe, the gradually evolved folkways or usages that in turn sustained and demarcated the union. It was a society that rested on primal instinct, foreordained by nature itself. The patriarchs, the elders, ruled over it, and one, possessing larger holdings or claiming a greater following of descendants or endowed with greater capacity or reputed prowess, became the chief.

So the tribe became rooted in its tribalism and developed the appropriate doctrines, including the legends of the fathers. Every tribe regarded itself as superior to the tribes without. Its blood was purer and nobler. Its locality was the center of the universe. Its ancestors were heroes and demigods. If the tribe was monotheistic, its god was the only true god. Similar sentiments still prevail among ourselves, no matter what the scale of our community. It is inherent in our conceptions of patriotism. And we have hymns that are not so remote from the ancestral faith.

> For all their gods are idols dumb
> That blinded nations fear.

Inevitably, under these conditions, a state of hostility or at least of mutual suspicion existed between tribe and tribe, with consequent raids and border forays. The logic of organization could not overcome the separatism of the tribal mores. The early indoctrination of the young, proceeding not from parents alone but from the ethos of the whole folk, is the strongest of all formative influences, indelibly stamped on the whole of life. It is rejected only under the continued pressures of drastic social change. It was not because of any general recognition of the benefits of the larger community that the tribal stage ended in various parts of the earth, but because conquests and annexations and occasionally the urgency of united defense against a more powerful enemy brought about the supertribal community, which became the country or the city-state, within which the sentiment of common membership, as subjects or citizens and later as nationals, took priority over the sentiment of the tribe.

One way in which the transcendence of the blood bond was achieved was through the rise of a city at some focal or strategic point. The city has always been a magnet that draws people into it from near and far. It thus becomes great enough to dominate a considerable hinterland. Situated in a naturally fortified position, or at a good haven for trading, or at some crossroads of communication, it became the capital of a region or gained the independence of a city-state. Such cities were cultural centers and they have had profound effects on the development of all later civilizations. Such was Ur and Babylon and Nineveh and Jerusalem and Troy and Knossos and Athens and Sparta and Corinth and Carthage and Tenochtitlan and Cuzco and many more besides. The city made men citizens, not kinsmen. The heterogeneity of the folk prevailed over the blood bond asserted by the patricians, the elite families. The bond of union was freer, more flexible, more inclusive, being a social and not primarily a biological bond. Hence it opened the possibility of still larger social unities.

Under certain conditions, and especially in the Orient, the enlarged society did not assume the form of a city-state, with its hinterland and colonies, but became a country or an empire of the feudal type under the rule of a kingly or an imperial court. Its people were subjects rather than citizens, mainly serfs attached to the land of their various overlords. It included numerous tribes, and common subjection and the rule of the inclusive law reduced to unimportance the aloofness and hostile violence between tribe and tribe. A common civilization took hold, and local and tribal usages accommodated themselves within a pervasive culture. The larger society, with its spreading communications, gave greatly increased opportunities for the development of the arts, of the luxuries and refinements of living, though it was only a small elite that enjoyed most of these benefits.

The coming of the supertribal community brought other changes in the place and role of physical power than its primary contribution, the expansion of the area within which disputes between group and group were settled otherwise than by resort to collective violence. Hitherto there was practically no distinction between law and custom. Now there was the law of the land, with its greater range and superior sanction, besides the variant customs of localities and tribes. The basis of obligation was broadened. Authority no longer rested on personal or familial relationships to chief or patriarch. You obeyed, no matter what your origin, tribe, or race, because you belonged within the territory where the law ran. Authority was thus magnified. The ruler was supreme, divinely appointed, invested with majesty.

On the other hand the greater range of internal peace, itself not wholly secure because of occasional attempts of regional overlords to gain the supreme power, increased also the range and the destructiveness of war between the new states or empires. The ambitions of rulers were whetted by their power. Now they were out for conquest. The prestige of military power increased as it came to be controlled by a permanent professional corps. As for the city-states, usually rather small territories neighbored by others of the same type, they were frequently at feud with their neighbors, and warfare was more the rule than the exception. Every leading city-state was at enmity with any rival. So, for example, Athens carried on a disastrous war with Sparta, and thus Greece became so weakened that it fell a rather easy prey first to Macedonia and then to Rome. Similarly in a later age the quarrelsome city-states of Italy became for several centuries the spoil of French and Austrian and Spanish invaders.

Warfare between the power systems of the enlarged communities was a very different affair from the sporadic clashes of tribal warfare. Power elites, with their greater resources and regular war establishments, planned and calculated for the expansion of their dominions. One consequence was the establishment of great empires. So in the Orient rose the Chinese Empire and in the Near East the empires of Assyria, Babylonia, Persia, and moving westward the empires of Macedonia and Turkey. Some city-states in their turn pursued imperial ambitions. Athens made an abortive attempt, and at length Rome greatly outpassed them all, creating the far-stretching Roman Empire. But empire, relying on the power of a metropolitan people over subject areas much larger in extent than itself, is inherently unstable, and empire succeeded empire in the unhappy kaleidoscope of history. Only the Chinese Empire has been able to resist for millennia the impact of divisive forces and achieve the lasting integration of a common culture, though Russia has been able to consolidate into one country most of its imperial annexations, establishing the conditions that may presage relatively permanent endurance. In the West the invaders who destroyed the Roman Empire, the Huns and the Goths, were unable to build up any substitute. After a time of confusions the feudal system with its loose-jointed seminominal empire was organized. It was many centuries later that with the breakup of feudalism the rising countries of the Atlantic seaboard, Spain and Portugal and Holland and England, created their own maritime empires, stretching far into Africa and the Orient and over the whole hemisphere that had hitherto remained outside the march of recorded history.

In sum, the first major stage in the transformation of power gave sheer might a far bigger historical role than before. On the surface at least, history became in large measure the story of how successive conquests overran local cultures and organized dynasties and empires, laying waste and destroying and rebuilding, defending and attacking, until the conquerors themselves became the victims of new-rising powers. But in the process, the insulation of numerous little tribes was broken and over large areas a common speech and common culture were established; and within these dominions, while they flourished, there were temporary spells of peace under law in which the creative drives of men found some degree of expression in achievements far more enduring than the conquests themselves.

Our second stage in the transformation of power was *the rise of the democratic principle*. For a long time it was a very precarious initiative, at first short-lived, then partially recovered, and thereafter disappearing until at length it redeveloped under conditions that led to its more enduring establishment. The word "democracy" was a fitting enough name for its earlier aspects. It meant the rule of the demos, the body of citizens, the "direct democracy" that prevailed in later fifth-century Athens, in the age of Pericles. Under it every citizen had in effect equal political opportunity and equal voting power. A whole series of changes in the distribution and equalization of power was involved. It meant a regular electoral sytem for the selection of state officials. It meant the abrogation of the rights of landownership and of rank and of ancestral privilege in the area of government. Nevertheless this remarkable system was very far from being a democracy, as we now understand the term. The Athenian demos, the privileged citizen corps of a relatively small city, constituted less than a third of the residents of the city. Citizenship was a privilege jealously reserved for the sons of freeborn Athenians, who ruled a city containing many resident aliens and also a large slave population. Actually its democracy was the rule of those citizens who were able to meet and spend long days in the marketplace, debating and passing on such matters as were prepared for submission to them by their Council. But it was certainly a unique experiment for its time. Other cities of the Hellenic world had assemblies on occasion, and we hear of meetings of the folk elsewhere to applaud or to protest against some decision or project of the rulers. But Athens alone had a fully articulated system for government by the demos itself. All the citizens, rich or poor, patrician or humble, general or tanner, had not only equal rights before the law but also equal right to run for office through citizen suffrage. So far did the passion for equality reach that some important offices were actually filled by lot.

Men rarely advance to new institutions because of any perception of their relation to the general welfare. It was not the love of democracy that brought into being the first salient democratic experiment. Athens was the center of the marvelous cultural flowering of Hellas. Its citizens had an unusually high educational level. Their protests and uprisings against the exactions of the propertied class caused such disturbances that a series of specially appointed legislators, Draco and Solon and Cleisthenes, were able to enact the constitutional changes that brought the demos into full power. The process was furthered by the demands of the veterans of Athens' successful wars, calling for landholdings and other rights. Democracy can never arise except among peoples who are alert and articulate about their needs. Even so, the

Athenian experiment in democracy was a highly precarious affair, endangered by power-hungry demagogues and cliques, regarded by all substantial folk as catering to the vulgar mob, mocked by satirists like Aristophanes, and roundly condemned by philosophers like Plato. Moreover, the slave basis on which the economy was built prevented both the development and the adequate recognition of the democratic creed.

Democracy in any form and on any scale inaugurates two great changes in the residence of power. Not only does it abrogate the political rights and the grosser coercions of an upper class but it also provides an orderly peaceful way of determining the headship and the major positions of responsibility within the system of government.

So revolutionary a change could not have been expected to make much headway in a world in which government had been wholly the prerogative of property and rank. The frequency of war created another grave peril, for war is inherently hostile to the democratic ethos. It was in fact the disastrous war between Athens and Sparta, the Peloponnesian War, that wrote the epitaph on the first great democratic experiment. A similar fate befell the next great approach to democracy, that of the Roman Republic, with its popularly elected magistrates, its tribunes of the people, and its assemblies of the various orders of the people. At Rome, however, it was not external foes but the rival ambitions of powerful proconsuls and generals, bringing about civil wars, that ended democracy with the principate of Augustus, the precursor of empire. Neither the Greeks nor the Romans had found a way to adjust the democratic machinery of a single city to the conditions of a greater territory. If you held the citizenship of Rome and lived in Greece or in Thrace, you still could not vote except in the comitia at Rome. This lack of political inventiveness militated against any democratic cohesion, and made the outmoded system the more insecure.

When at length the Roman Empire fell before the invading "barbarians," many centuries had to pass before the democratic experiment was revived. It was in the city that democracy always had been bred, and the city was wholly subordinate under the feudal system. In the course of the Middle Ages, various cities regained a virtual independence, and it was there, in the republican cities of Italy, of Flanders, and of Germany, that the next democratic movements arose. They had one important advantage over Athens and Rome. Lacking the drag of slave labor, democracy could now begin to take a fuller significance, as a vindication of human rights. The principle itself was supported by the Christian doctrine that all men were made alike in the image of God. But the implementation of the principle remained very limited.

The new Western monarchies that broke out of feudalism were the first lands in which a more stable form of democracy developed, a democracy embracing a nation, not merely the burgesses of some flourishing city, a democracy not exhibited merely in town meetings of the citizen body but in parliaments where the elected representatives of the people sat. It was a slow development, with occasional setbacks. The demands of increasingly prosperous elements of the middle class won a franchise that broadened out, first in England and then in Western Europe, into a fuller democracy. Then with the rise of the new industrial machinery, the working classes learned to organize and to utilize their hitherto latent power so as to obtain a practically universal franchise. The last stage of this process has been the political enfranchisement of women.

So in the Western world, embracing the greater West with the establishment of the American republic, democracy came into its own, spreading also into some other countries across the world. It is a system of government that is always imperfect, never attaining to the full realization of its principle, but one that has meant, wherever it has been effectively established, the most complete transformation of the ancient order of power, substituting consent for coercion, equality of rights for arbitrary controls in the regulation of the political concerns of the whole nation, and giving a new dignity to the once powerless by conferring on them in full measure a right that formerly was the prerogative of birth and wealth. The right was also a power, one that became an instrument in the reshaping of the entire hierarchy of social powers.

Another stage in the transformation of power had been imperceptibly advancing long before the developments just recorded but did not reach its culmination before the latter half of the nineteenth century. This was *the liberation of mankind from slavery*. We noted that the greater civilizations of ancient times had a slave basis. In effect, all the hard toil was done by servile labor. Besides the slaves proper there were the serfs, peasants bound to the soil and virtually helpless to resist the exactions and tyrannies of the landowners. Slavery itself began to be reduced in scale through the process of manumission, which was greatly expanded during the period of the Roman Empire. The social demoralization of the system of slavery became particularly serious with the development under the Roman Empire of the *latifundia*, great landholdings run by slave labor and displacing the former yoemen or farmers. Gradually slavery in agriculture was replaced by serfdom, a kind of bondage under which men retained a precarious degree of personal freedom so long as they supplied the services and met the quotas of production demanded by the land-holders. In the Middle Ages serfdom extended over the whole range of feudal society.

As America became colonized, slavery was revived on a great scale by the European invaders. The colonial slave trade was initiated in the fifteenth century by the Portuguese and then taken up by Spanish, Dutch, and British traders. Africa was ransacked for slaves. African chiefs themselves dealt freely in slaves, and prisoners captured in their wars were regularly enslaved for that purpose. It was not until near the end of the eighteenth century that the horrors of the slave trade created the movement for its abolition associated with the name of William Wilberforce, and soon thereafter the transport of slaves was prohibited for British and American vessels. Slavery was altogether renounced by the chief countries of Europe, but it needed the Civil War to end the "peculiar institution" in the Southern United States. By 1888, when Brazil abolished it, the American continent knew it no more.

Africa, from which millions of slaves have been recruited and within which virtual slavery has lingered on in certain colonial areas, was the last continent to share the surge of the movement for human rights that is now promising to end what remains of the chattel treatment of human beings.

Slavery, then, has disappeared as an institution, and serfdom has over great areas either been abolished or has dwindled away. It would seem that the arbitrary power that turned men into the will-less instruments of other men has run its course. Dominations of many kinds persist, but this rankest form of it was inevitably doomed in the process of the inclusive system of transformations with which we are here concerned.

All of these transformations of power have moved in the same direction. They have abolished or reduced certain forms of sheer subjection, based on ancestral rights, on class distinctions, on property ownership, and on racial dominance. A great series of interrelated historical changes, the growth of urbanization, technological advances in the art of war, in the modes of production, in communication and trade, the consequent reorganizations of the social order, the growth of scientific knowledge and its impacts on society, the dissolution of ancient customary ways under the frictions of populational mobility, and so forth, have lain back of changes in the attitudes and aspirations of the peoples and in their potentialities for pursuing them.

The latest of these transformations has been *the dissolution of colonial empire*. In the past, empire was the only form of large-scale political unification beyond the city-state and the nation-state. Some great land empires, especially China and Russia, found it possible to consolidate their conquests and become in time expanded unitary states with a more or less pervasive culture. The maritime empires were a different case. They ruled over great distances an array of peoples of diverse races and cultures. No cohesion was possible under these conditions. Certain colonial areas mainly inhabited by immigrant citizens of the metropolitan country became practically independent countries; the others continued to be held by superior might. Half the earth had become the possession of the maritime powers. The discovery of America opened up a whole continent to the exploitation of the Spanish and the Portuguese. The British and the French followed and took possession of the expanses of North America, though the French lost most of it in wars with the British, and made deals with them and then with the United States for the transfer of other parts. The British and the French and the Dutch seized vast areas in Africa, in the Orient, and in the Pacific sector. Finally, in the industrial competition of the later nineteenth century, there came a great scramble on the part of the Western powers and also of Japan, with Germany belatedly joining in, to annex whatever industrially undeveloped areas remained exposed to seizure.

During the nineteenth century there were already signs that the heyday of colonial empire might be passing. Within its first half, Latin America, with its Western European culture basis, responded to the surge of nationalism by uprisings that liberated its various countries from the weakening grasp of Spain and Portugal; elsewhere in colonial areas there were occasional disturbances and growing unrest. In the metropolitan countries themselves there was some questioning concerning the presumptive economic benefits of empire, and, as troubles within them increased, concerning the military advantage of certain of these possessions.

It was, however, the twentieth century that witnessed the great dissolution of empire. The shock of two world wars, the employment of colonial soldiery, the wresting of colonies from the defeated countries and the placing of them under mandate or trust, the European-trained or American-trained natives of colonial areas who become the promoters of new policies in the colonies, the growing difficulty of resisting independence movements owing to the jealousies between the Soviet area and the West, these and related forces gave enormous impetus to the nationalistic surge. Once the spirit of nationalism is really stirred, it cannot be stayed and can be checked—for a time—only at heavy cost. The result has been that the empires of Britain and France and Holland have gone the way of the empire of Spain, except that the British and the French have learned to salvage some cooperative tie between themselves and many of their former dependencies. A few powers have refused to accept the inexorable process, like Portugal in

Angola and the Union of South Africa in its parlous position in the midst of colored subject peoples of various origins.

In earlier times empires passed away, only to be succeeded by new empires. In our time, empires have been passing away in a quite different manner, for their territories, over Africa and Asia and the islands of the oceans, have become nations in their own right, a development that is new in human history. And they all became members of the United Nations, safeguarded by one another as well as by the jealousies of rival superpowers.

A curious feature of the present situation, though it too is probably doomed by the larger trend of the times, is the disguised empire that the most vocal of all the anti-imperialist propagandists has set up, the satellite *imperium* of Soviet Russia. It includes the numerous smaller states fringing the length of its eastern border. Some—Lativia, Lithuania, and Estonia——have been simply incorporated within its main territory. Others, the more important group, including Poland, Czechoslovakia, Hungary, Rumania, Bulgaria, and Albania, have become satellites under puppet Communist Party heads, dominating the only party that is permitted to exist. These so-called "people's states" are impelled to follow the Party line, especially in their foreign relations, and any popular movement for freedom is treated as rebellion, the most flagrant case being the bloody suppression with the aid of Russian tanks of the Hungarian uprising. The urge for independence cannot, however, be suppressed. Yugoslavia successfully dared to differ with Russia on Communist policies, as Albania is doing in degree at the time of writing. Poland has taken a different line and has been able to assert some measure of cultural freedom, greater or less as the conditions have admitted. Hungary has again made advances in the same direction.

We have reviewed four interrelated long-trend social processes, each of which has limited or abolished the power of status-occupying groups to coerce at their will other groups that lacked this status. These processes transformed the power structure in several ways; first, by leveling out some gross disparities of power; second, by conferring new powers on those who had hitherto been relatively powerless, political powers such as the right to vote or the right to unionize; and third, by giving new play to non-coercive powers that had been previously limited by coercive controls, making possible the "career open to talents" and widening the opportunities through the access to knowledge and to training in the arts.

In our own day a great breakthrough in science has created the necessity for a new and climactic reduction in the role of physical coercion. The stupendous violence of the thermonuclear bomb presents the great powers of the earth with a final dilemma, either to renounce international war or to destroy themselves beyond redemption by resorting to it. A third possibility, an agreement to jettison atomic weapons and still fight wars but with "conventional" armaments, would be altogether too precarious an arrangement, since the know-how of the bomb can never be obliterated. When at length the great powers accept the inevitable conclusion—assuming that no combination of bluff and folly, negligence and mechanical accident first unlooses the holocaust —the era of international wars on the great scale will end in some established system of world regulation.

This consummation, of momentous importance as it would be, would by no means bring a complete assurance of international peace. There would still be rifts and serious disturbances within the international system, and the danger of secession and fatal division would still exist. But it would be a reasonable hope that once international law was established it would build up so many sustaining interests and influences that, as lesser unifications have done in the past, it would overcome these perils. There would still, however, be outbreaks of sporadic violence, border raids and forays, especially between lesser states, the overthrow of governments by internal insurrections, and processes of subversion that illicitly use some coercive device. The impulse to use physical force is native to human beings, as native as the ambition and hate and injured pride that prompt it. Young boys are prone to bully and torment the weaker among them, and while the discipline of growing up holds the tendency in leash it by no means eradicates it. Were it not for the criminal law, there would be enough violence and spoliation to make civil existence intolerable. The lack of international law now endangers all human existence, and the consensus of the peoples in its favor is practically as great as the consensus that upholds the law of the land.

It is conceivable that some relatively powerful dissident government might refuse to adhere to the general pact establishing international law as the final authority in the settlement of disputes between nations. The likelihood that this rejection would happen, or if so would persist for any length of time, is lessened if we consider the formidable efficacy of the economic and other sanctions that would inevitably be applied.

But we have as a warning the present utterly intransigent position of the Chinese government, which refuses to accept the feasibility of peaceful coexistence between Marxist and capitalist countries, and insists that even nuclear war may be a necessary and desirable alternative. While this assertion is made in the name of the sacred ideology, there can be little doubt that, in this case as in so many others, the front of ideology is a pseudo-mask for the pursuit of power. It is directed not against the West but against the stronger comrade country that is refusing to gratify China's appetite for more power. It is not the statement of a purpose, but a formula of defiance.

However this may be, we can be certain that the definitive establishment of international law will create a multitude of new problems that only long and troubled negotiations can mitigate. No great advance is accomplished without travail, and though the costs must be paid there develops under it a new orientation that is likely to change the whole course of the future.

Moreover, this prospective consummation, the outlawing of physical force for the settlement of international disputes, would be the culmination of the agelong process that incorporated the kindred and the tribe in the people, the community, the nation, gave new cohesion to the community by turning its members into citizens, dissolved the might-sustained structure of empire so that its components could find their unity as free peoples—and thus prepared the ground for the community of nations. Every step in this process was taken under the strong impulsion of conditions that rendered the alternative of the *status quo ante* either impossible or exceedingly undesirable—and the same impulsion is upon us again. The road of civilization was not built because people appreciated in advance the benefits of civilization but because of the intolerable evils they would suffer unless they proceeded with it.

12.

The Shifting Patterns
of Social Power

As we have seen, where the range of sheer physical coercion is curtailed, the role of other forms of power is increased. Where physical coercion is the prime instrument of authority, where authority owes no responsibility, no accountability, to those whom it controls, the spiritual impulses and the intellectual drives within a people are suppressed, the fine arts are cramped because they must cater to the interest and the limitations of the patron-masters, and the functional capacities of many potential contributors to the service of society remain underdeveloped. The greater the area of arbitrary authority the less is the freedom available to the intrinsic powers of men's minds and hearts.

Many changes in the texture of society and in the controls that advancing technology provided for the greater utilization of resources combined with concomitant and responsive changes in the ideologies of men and groups to bring about the recession of

173

arbitrary power. In the present chapter we shall review the manner in which, within our modern civilization and particularly with the more flexible systems of modern society that we rather loosely designate the "free world," preeminence or priority is constantly passing from one to another among the various forms of social power. And between these powers themselves coalitions and divorces, attractions and repulsions combine to make the social scene as changeful as the surface of the sea.

Let us first point up the contrast between the power structure of a European feudal society and that of our own. In the former there was a determinate and stable hierarchy. The grading ran from the monarchy through the various orders of nobility to the lesser gentry (the knights and squires), and a nearly impassable gap separated all these from the commonalty with their minor ratings down to the serf. While in our society function is an independent source of power that to a very large extent can be achieved without regard to prior social status, in the feudal society function was an attribute of rank and rank itself an attribute of birth. The upper class, from the great duke to the local squire, were mostly concerned with controlling and administrating the areas of which they were the owners or the overlords and keeping in order the people of their domains by the rough justice they meted out. Some of their members entered the service of the king as courtiers, statesmen, or military officers. Some were patrons of the arts, employing painters, musicians, architects, sculptors, and workers in the luxury crafts. There was also the church, which accommodated itself to the lines of the establishment, its higher dignitaries—cardinals and bishops—being usually themselves landowners of considerable rank. The lords spiritual ranged alongside the secular lords.

In the upper ratings of the commonalty came the stewards and

supervisors of the great estates, the professionals, particularly law-
yers, who also were mostly employed by the upper class, and an
occasional financier who was serviceable to the nobility. Trades-
men usually had a lower rating, though in the antifeudal cities
guilds of merchants and of craftsmen broke through the barriers
to some power and dignity. As for women, they were almost
wholly excluded from power and office, unless they were queens,
though an occasional duchess or countess could wield considerable
influence. Aside from the duties of the household and the drudgery of the field, the only office open to women in general was to
be the mistress of a gentleman or, on the lowest reach, a prostitute.

Under such conditions centuries might pass over a region and
the social order remain essentially unchanged, unless some devastating invasion swept through it.

Now, in a modern democracy, we have no such tier-on-tier
pyramid in which all men have their appointed stations. Instead,
the skyline of power somewhat resembles that of one of our great
cities, with numerous peaks and turrets, a skyline that never remains the same over any length of years. We have numerous
semi-independent foci of power, centered in great functional organizations, uninhibited by class lines or preassigned status, combating one another when their respective interests collide, fluctuating in strength as new developments emerge out of the ceaseless
activity of science-based technology and evoke new social and
cultural responses. In this melee, lesser categories advance, to
threaten and overtop previously major ones, and the ordering of
the whole society rests on the shifting adjustments that determine
the compromises between contending forces. The will of the state
itself may at points be thwarted and challenged by a labor union or
a syndicate of corporations. Or it may have to accept a compromise with a group representing high finance. It may be resisted by

a dissident minority, as has been the case in the United States since the antisegregation ruling was handed down. And when we say "the state" we are referring to a complex of separate powers that at times are so seriously at odds as to deadlock legislative and administrative decisions. It is all a ceaseless welter of conflict and struggle, with new dominances rising from time to time, but some *modus vivendi,* some compromise, is nearly always reached, and in the last resort there is the appeal to the verdict of public opinion.

The struggle is one of policymakers as well as of policies. The policymakers have three not always compatible objectives, and the respective weight they attach to each is an index of the quality of their leadership. They are concerned to increase the power and prestige of their various organizations, whether they be political, economic, technological, cultural, philanthropic, recreational, or other. They want to promote the function to which the organization is dedicated, whether it be to produce more or better goods and in any event to show higher profits, or to strengthen some party or advance some cause, or to assure better public service in the particular area of their interest, or so forth. And they want to advance their personal prestige and power and usually their own economic prosperity. The first and third of these objectives are in reasonably good accord, but the first may be, and the third not infrequently is, at variance with the second.

In addition to the power competition between organizations, there are various other bases of power struggle within the complex freedoms of a modern society, notably local and regional bases. Sometimes the struggle is due to conflicting or competing interests, sometimes it is for prestige or for priority, sometimes over moral or moralistic issues between, say, the large city and the hinterland, since the city tends to draw the young people of the countryside to itself and is regarded as following modes of life that the less urbanized areas do not favor. Often the rural areas have a different cultural outlook, a more conservative spirit, which animates political opposition in state and regional councils. There are also large-scale regional interests that wage campaigns against what they regard as the opposing interests of other areas, as exemplified by the organizations of Middle Western farming interests that have frequently denounced the financial interests of "Wall Street." In broad terms, every special interest—and the number is legion—organizes for defense and for attack against some other special interest or interests.

In this seething world of conflicts for place and dominance, certain trends emerge that indicate the continuous adjustment of the whole social order to developments in the underlying technology and the sustaining culture of the age. Of particular significance is the rise of new functions to dominate over or take the place of old ones, thus creating a succession of power elites almost wholly absent from earlier society.

The primary change that inaugurated this new sequence in leadership was the development of mechanized industry. The owners of the new factories, mostly self-made men of the middle class, began to amass profits that gave them social leverage to assert themselves against the establishment of the landed gentry, and sometimes impoverished members of the latter class were ready to ally themselves through marriage with the new rich. The ancient unity of birth and wealth had already been weakened by the advancement of the middle class, the more enterprising members of which had made good in trade, commerce, shipping, and finance. But the rapid growth of the textile industries under the new conditions introduced the age in which great industrialists became more potent in the economy than landed proprietors.

The owners controlled their mills, their plants of various kinds. They were personally in charge of their affairs. Frequently ownership remained vested in families, and the top management descended from father to son or to some near relatives of the original owners. But as the scale of industry increased, as the machinery of production became more elaborate and more expensive, and as in the increasing competitive struggle some owners lost out and the more successful ones took over the business, a new development opened up that drastically changed the basis and the character of economic power. The increasing magnitude of operation and the greater outlays necessary for successful competition because of the rapid obsolescence of machinery, the size and variety of inventories, and so forth, made it difficult, often impossible, and generally undesirable, to carry the business on under individual ownership. Moreover, management itself was becoming so complex that it called for experts in that art, and often the owners did not qualify. There were also certain legal advantages and economic safeguards in the conversion of private businesses into corporations. Unlike individual concerns and partnerships, corporations were, as the French style them, "anonymous," owned by a diversity of shareholders who knew for the most part little or nothing about the property they owned. As shareholders, they did not own concrete properties, such as diesel engines or blast furnaces or turbines or paper mills or natural gas pipelines, but only certain titles to financial benefits, share certificates having a market value and yielding dividends determined by the directors when the business was prosperous enough.

Thus in all the greater industrial, commercial, and financial enterprises, management has become separated from ownership and taken over most of the former powers of ownership. Only in rare instances has any great enterprise remained under the direct control of the original family which initiated the business, as the Ford Company succeeded in doing for a time. Corporate management is vested in a board whose members usually own a very small percentage of the stock that represents the assets of the corporation. And legal ownership is scattered among thousands of people across the country or even across the world. They own a collective possession which most of them have never seen, and, while they have the right to appoint the directors of it, they are so remote from the whole operation that usually all they do is sign proxies in favor of the list of directors annually submitted to them.

Formerly there were two kinds of property, public and private. Now there are three, corporate property being a kind of intermediate between the other two. Corporate property is not private as a man's house and garden are private. Its legal owners are amorphous. They cannot use it or occupy it and they do not control it. The composition of ownership changes every day as shares are bought and sold in the market. Corporate property is, as property, impersonal, property held in trust for owners mostly unknown to the trustees. It is obvious, therefore, that the management of these great undertakings, some of them ranging into the billion-dollar bracket, is a new power of vast magnitude in our present-day society. It is a power that has continued to expand in scale of operations since the changeover to corporate control took hold in the nineteenth century. Now corporations and fiduciary trusts of many kinds dominate the economic field.

The vast power exercised by management, in which we may here include both the active directors on boards and the major executives who are responsible to them, created new economic and political problems. It was a kind of power unknown to the world before, this power of private citizens to control and manipulate other people's goods and other people's money with practically no supervision by these people themselves, a power that involved only a limited responsibility so that if the enterprise went bankrupt it did not directly involve the private purses of the management. It was, moreover, the power of a corporation that had no term to its existence, that might endure through centuries and was potentially immortal. And it was also a rather lucrative power, especially for the top executives, who were rewarded by substantial salaries, supplemented often by stock options, bonuses, ample retirement provision, expense accounts, and other fringe benefits.

So great a power was bound, in the many-peaked society of our times, to evoke checks on it of some sort. One of these came from the rise of another new power. While the managerial class was gaining hold over the wide fields of industry, trade, commerce, finance, communications, public utilities, and newspaper publishing—and, in a less conspicuous way, in the great welfare organizations and foundations—the trade-union movement was making great headway. Their leaders were masterful men who had the personality, the forthrightness, the energy, and the persuasiveness to rise to the top, and once there they were frequently able to retain their position over lengthy periods, if not for life. They possessed one of the most formidable of social weapons, the power to call a strike—most rarely would the union members refuse to ratify this strategy—and in so doing to cripple a large area of the industrial life. The ample funds raised as union dues and the cooperative attitude of other unions enabled them to make the strike so much the more effective. In the face of this power, government itself has frequently to mediate between the two sides in the endeavor to reestablish the peace, and it resorts to various other devices, such as the insistence on a temporary truce. In a democratic society government fears to make drastic laws forbidding strikes that constitute not only a serious hardship for the public but also a danger to the economy. There is, however, a danger point at which any government will intervene to end the dispute, though there is much difference of opinion on the mechanism of control and the point where it must be exercised. In the present context, however, we are merely pointing out that the power of the labor union is a quite positive check on the power of management.

In recent times management has been confronted also by additional governmental controls. In some industrial countries business has over a relatively long period been restrained by laws forbidding monopolistic tendencies. It has also been limited by regulations prescribing minimum wages, hygienic and safety measures, and more recently by a series of requirements arising out of social security legislation. Such controls, however, remained peripheral to the main activities of business enterprise. It was as a consequence of the occurrence of sharp depressions, spurred by the widespread unemployment and misery they caused, that governments which previously had taken a somewhat laissez-faire position were impelled into the business of economic planning. In the United States the Federal Reserve System, with its power to raise or lower the discount rate, became in effect a planning agency. Taxing policy was also to some extent guided by consideration of the relative effect on the economy of various modes of raising governmental revenues as well as of higher or lower tax rates in general.

In the United States the most direct head-on clash between the policy of government and that of a particular industry occurred when the steel industry, on the initiative of the United States Steel Corporation, raised its prices at a time when the government was making determined efforts to stay inflation and after it had used its influence with the steel union to accept a new contract that provided for no actual wage increase. The pressures the government brought to bear on the industry proved quickly effective and the price rise was rescinded. This dramatic affair showed up the fact that the power of government extends well beyond its legislative authority and its executive rulings. It gives out large-scale contracts for all kinds of commodities, raw materials, and services, contracts on the granting of which the success or lack of success of many firms depend. It is the greatest employer of labor and the greatest purchaser of its products. It has a colossal budget, vastly beyond the range of any corporation or group of corporations. Its patronage, ramifying through every area of the country, makes millions of persons directly or indirectly beholden to it. Through a number of commissions and boards, whose members are its appointees, it regulates traffic by road and rail and air, assigns the channels of television and radio communication, arranges the tariff rates that affect the whole import and export trade, controls the rate-making of public utilities, decides whether mergers or combines or price-fixing agreements are infringements of the antimonopoly legislation, and so forth. No corporation or group of corporations can afford for long to flout such a panoply of power.

On the other side we must add that no democratic government can afford to incur the concerted opposition of the business world if it thereby alienates any considerable body of its supporters. Franklin Roosevelt encountered very widespread and vehement business opposition, but he carried his program through owing to his large majority and to the deepness of the depression.

Since power in the modern world has become dominantly functional—that is, more and more detached from prior status, descent, class, or ethnic distinctions, and more attached to office achieved through competitive struggle or as a recognition of competence in former service—it is not surprising that changes in the ranking of one form of power as against another should be rather frequent. The one main limitation of this trend is that wealth has considerable influence, directly and indirectly, on the selection of those appointed to high-rated functions. The valuation of one function as against another varies in accord with social and technological change. The ranking of the managerial class has been limited by new countering forces, aside from governmental controls and the demands of the trade unions. Other checks on it spring from the need for professional experts to guide the development and the operation of the increasingly complex mechanism of production. Such professionals are no longer mere outsiders who are called in to give technical advice on particular points. In the age of the computer, of automation, of nuclear energy, of Telstar and of "wonder drugs," the industrial engineer, the electronics expert, the research chemist, the biochemist, the biologist, the atomic physicist must direct new developments and propose new directions. The research laboratories of the great corporations are no longer ancillary services; they are essential features of the whole operation, and their staffs are given a practical independence in the way they conduct their researches. Management has to share its responsibility with others for many of its most important decisions.

A not dissimilar situation now holds in certain areas of government. Professional experts have important roles in the planning of overall economic policy and in such matters as budgeting, banking, and taxation. Atomic physicists have a primary place in the planning undertaken in the Atomic Energy Commission and beyond that in the military programs of the country. The Rand Corporation, government-financed, invites political and social scientists and other scholars to devote themselves within its retreat to the consideration of the problems of strategy and general administration. When the weapons of warfare were relatively simple mechanisms, the professional soldiers could be presumed to appreciate their role in military strategy, their potentials for defense and offense, and possibly the political consequences of their effective use. But now that the arsenal of war has become so incredibly destructive, the main objective of military power can be no longer the ability to fight successful wars but the maintenance of a potential so geared and poised that it will deter any nuclear-armed enemy from any rational hope of knocking out in advance the ruinous counteraction of the defense. (Even to state such an objective is to suggest how curiously the realities of the new power defeat all the traditional conceptions of power politics and raise problems that can be resolved only by the radical acceptance of a novel kind of realism.) In any event, considerations of strategy are no longer the prerogative solely of the military staff, since they depend so much on the interpretation of the attitudes and the policies of rival powers. There is indeed a mystique about such calculations that wavers between rationality and irrationality.

One consequence of these developments is the emergence of a new group, a special category of politico-military strategists composed of political scientists, publicists, political economists, and such like, some of whom find favor in high places and share directly or indirectly in the policymaking process. Together with governmental strategists, they have reduced significantly the role of the old-time military staff strategists. If, for example, a certain type of bomber or of medium-range missile is discontinued, it is quite likely to be on the advice of the new experts and is not unlikely to be in the face of opposition from the regular military staff or some branch of it.

Perhaps the most important aspect of the new changefulness

in the priorities of power we have been describing is not so much the decline or supersession of older functions in favor of new ones as the rise of so many new functions of much social significance. Our survey has by no means included all of these. There are also the leaders in the profession of persuasion, that is, the advertising experts and the public relations men, the owners of the great newspaper chains, and we might include also the glamor entertainers and the heroes of the mass spectator sports.

A society in which function is more prestigeful than inheritance or prescriptive right is inevitably one in which the ranking of power priorities is unstable. It is one in which over any length of time innovating tendencies are likely to prevail over conservative tendencies. It has less respect not only for tradition but for the great achievements of the past. Its culture is unstable and somewhat amorphous. At the one extreme are groups that seek not only to modify but wholly to reject established ways of doing or thinking in favor of bold breakaway experiments. This tendency is particularly manifested in various artistic circles, so that the new age, the age that began yesterday, is acclaimed in music, painting, sculpture, dramatic and literary forms. At the other extreme there is the larger minority who yearn for what they regard as the good old days. But that yearning is vain so long as function usurps the former prerogative of status. The only really stable society is one in which function, no matter how significant, is subordinated to prior status, to the rights of an established class and the inheritance of power. Many of us, especially as we grow old, hanker after a social firmament conformable to our habituations, to the adaptations we have learned to make and the familiar assurances we cherish, but the forces that our society has released are not to be stayed, for better or for worse.

Throughout the above discussion we have been thinking

mainly of the more democratic type of industrial society. But the displacement of prior status by function has also been a feature of the new communistic societies, though with a highly significant qualification. Marxist Communism proclaimed the abolition not only of prior status, that is, status dependent on birth, inheritance, or other factors aside from the personal qualities of the possessor, but of status altogether, status dependent on service or merit. The former type was to be abolished by the Communist Revolution, the second by the fulfillment of Communism in the classless society. Communism did abolish the old class system, the prerogatives of inherited rank and inherited wealth. The consummation that was to follow was, however, a pious myth, designed to give idealistic overtones to Communist realism. Function is always a source of power, whether the function is assigned on the basis of inheritance or wealth or connections or election or nomination. Function, being graded power, will create a class system by itself. Moreover, since Communism is founded on a specific creed, a secular theology that pronounces not only on the whole past course of human history but also on its future, and since the Party is conceived of as the authoritative exponent, guardian, and implementer of the articles of the creed, its political establishment jealously guards against any trends of opinion that might directly or indirectly contravene any tenet of the faith. Thus the Soviet system has some aspects of the fixity of a theocracy. Authority is enthroned, creating a status that is superior to function.

On the other hand the Soviet Union is an industrialized state with an advanced technology, which we saw to mean rather continuous change in functional priorities, and that in turn involves both a considerable social mobility and corresponding changes in social attitudes. In short, there is, to use a Marxist expression, a contradiction between the fixity of the creed and the experimental flexibility imposed by industrial change. This contradiction has had important repercussions on the Soviet system, right up to its authoritarian summit. The political setting and the political program have undergone vast changes since the early twenties. Ideological commissars no longer dictate to the big industrial managers. A rather elaborate class structure, based on function and changing with the times, has developed. Stalinism, once part of the sacrosanct canon, has been downgraded. Peaceful coexistence with capitalism has been proclaimed a desirable and even necessary policy. Nationalism has become more of a driving force in politics than Marxism. The rift with Communist China, which claims to be more Marxist than the Russian inheritors, is having a subtle influence in lessening the propagandist value of the ideology. One way or another there has been some reduction of the sharp demarcation between both the character and the interests of Soviet state-capitalism and of Western socio-capitalism.

A common technology is moving ahead all across the earth, and the easy and swift communication that is one of its products is gradually lessening the barriers of cultural alienation between regions near and far. The formerly subject peoples are already mostly independent and rising in the power scale. The trends in the basis and the distribution of power we have been describing in this and the previous chapter are now worldwide, at one or another stage of advancement. We are passing into some kind of world society with some degree of world order, bringing new dominances, new troubles, and new prospects within the forever unstable equilibrium of powers.

13.

Temptations and Failings of the Mighty

Power, we have pointed out, is of itself the neutral agency of all change and of all stability. In human society it is the means of all the desires and designs of men, of all their values and all their achievements. Being indifferent to the uses to which it is put, it has been a dangerous possession, the more dangerous the greater it is. It is dangerous insofar as the holder of power, of any of the forms of social power, separates his interest from the interests of other men. One form of social power, the power to govern, the power to command the services of others, to make them the instruments of another's will, has been the source of vast devastation and suffering throughout human history, though it has also been capable of great constructive developments. What makes this type of power the more dangerous is the liability to miscalculate that has so frequently attended its use.

So we turn to the question that lay back of Part One, the

answer to which can at best highlight a now obvious necessity. Why is unharnessed might so subject to the rash blunders and follies that have bedeviled mankind throughout the mostly inglorious record of the bloodstained government of man? The question assumes that the men of might have shown themselves more liable to serious error than the men who are experienced in conducting other important affairs. The reader must decide whether the answer we give to the question justifies the assumption on which the question is based.

The great ones of the earth have risen to the summit in various ways. Some have fought upward in the hidden strife of factions, and by their intrigues and strength of personality have reached their goal. Some, usually possessing an initial advantage, because of birth or wealth or favorable position, have known how to make successful appeals to the people or to the people's representatives, in the successive stages of their climb to the top. Some, a diminished few, were born to occupy an ancestral throne, though the decisive role may rest in the hands of their chief ministers. When the rulers are elected directly or indirectly by the people, the policies of the summit are still not determined by the electors. For in foreign relations official decisions are made behind the scenes, under conditions that are not exposed to the public, except for such information as they are fed from above.

Such rulers have surely had much experience in the conduct of affairs and in the behavior of human beings. Yet they have too frequently used their power in ways that proved to be not only unwise but freighted with disaster. Nor can it be said that the situations they faced were so difficult that such blunders were hard to avoid or that their potential consequences were unforeseeable. It would seem that some further explanation is called for.

It is our argument that a major part of the explanation lies in

the psychology of power, the kind of power that gives men rulership over multitudes. The possession of such power, and in many
cases the process of winning it, has an important effect on the
mind of the possessor. Holding a superior position, having risen
above other men, he becomes imbued with his sense of superiority.
He is surrounded by his servants and his sycophants. Decisions of
vital importance hang on his word. Superior in status, he is certainly inferior in knowledge to those who serve him, inferior in
the skills they put at his disposal, often inferior in wisdom, but
his higher status tends to make him regard these other attributes
as secondary, merely instrumental to the greater quality of rank.

Have we not known of persons who had worked with efficiency
and restraint in a subordinate role but who, when appointed to
the head position, seemed to undergo a change of personality
and became arrogant and domineering? Have we not known or
heard of persons who made a substantial success in the competitive world of affairs, and being thus free to turn their energies to
other fields took a leading role in some welfare organization or
other public service where they exhibited attitudes of self-asser-
tion and intolerance, riding roughshod over the advice of those
who had vastly more experience than themselves? Power is a
heady drink for many men, and not least for those who suffer
from a secret sense of inferiority.

The love of power is also the love of prestige, and that cherished accompaniment of power is itself a strong temptation to
error. To admit one is mistaken, to defer one's judgment to that
of others diminishes one's prestige, at least one's conception of it.
Consequently the ruler tends to give inadequate consideration to
any counsel he receives that is not in accord with his own views.
He is in especial tempted to act too precipitately in complex situations when it is important that the problem be viewed dispas-

sionately and from all sides, or in situations where the evidence on which action should be based is not yet all assembled. If the maintenance of prestige is prized by the ruler in domestic affairs, it is even more so in foreign relationships. Now the head of the government is concerned to uphold not only his own prestige but the prestige of his country. And this concern, proper enough in its own place, may be an impediment to effective negotiation, even in matters of critical importance. It is sometimes hard to distinguish between the maintenance of prestige and the stiffness of an inconsiderate pride.

The fear of the loss of face, or prestige, is sometimes carried to ironical extremes. Shakespeare makes Hamlet comment on "the imminent death of twenty thousand men" who go to fight over a worthless bit of land, "an eggshell," a little plot "which is not tomb enough and continent to hide the slain"—but "honor's at the stake." So, for nothing but face, great states have refused to reach agreements that would greatly benefit them alike, and the vaporous prestige they respectively sought is remembered no more. We may find something of this attitude in some of the abortive earlier negotiations between the United States and Soviet Russia over the issue of nuclear testing, each side making disproportionate conditions that the other side could not or obviously would not accept, and one side or the other being too ready to reject overtures from its adversary lest it seem to be yielding ground. In a similar spirit, though there the cause was merely frivolous, medieval knights scrapped to defend the honor of a lady which did not need and could not benefit by such defense. To enhance its cultural prestige, Soviet Russia has in its journals made numerous claims to the priority of Russians—in the days before Communism was heard of—in the discovery of great inventions and in the enunciation of famous theories for which credit is given in the historical record to Europeans or Americans. Not infrequently, on our part, when the Russians have achieved some space exploit that outdistanced any we had thus far made, our official statements have tended to minimize it as no significant advance over what we ourselves have accomplished. These are examples of minor foibles, but in other respects the competition for prestige becomes inordinately expensive, as in the race to put the first men on the moon, or perilous, as in the drive to be ahead in the quest for bigger or better annihilating bombs as a preliminary to any agreement for the abolition of nuclear tests.

The assertion of superiority to which the possession of high power prompts is not only adverse to successful negotiation but also tends to make the powerholder underestimate the difficulties of the policy he favors. We have already suggested that high power inclines its owner to pay less regard than it deserves to the counsel of others. With this double handicap it is not surprising that many opportunities for effective negotiation have been squandered, even where peace and war were in the balance.

The same lack of adequate consideration frequently affects the dealings of great states with small, weak, or backward ones. Here the sense of superiority is unchecked by counterclaims, and so it seems the less necessary for the strong to inquire closely into the problems of their prospective policies toward these peoples. Even when it has honestly sought to give them aid, the United States has at times failed to consider the conditions under which such aid could best advance their economic well-being; the mode of its distribution necessary to prevent its going into the wrong pockets; the repercussions it might have, unless precautions were taken, on their wage scales, on the native export trade, on their standards of living, and on their social morale. In these respects we have learned some lessons through unhappy experiences but not always in time to undo the damage. Occasionally the United States has acted toward newly created nations as though they could and should become democracies like ourselves, as though what was good for us was necessarily good for them. We have not sufficiently understood that a democracy is the slow birth of time and cannot be created overnight. Sometimes we have put pressures on them to give up being neutral and align themselves with us in the Cold War—certainly a proper desire on our part, but one that is not effectively advanced by pressure.

Another kind of miscalculation arises from the assumption of the powerful, in their dealing with weaker peoples, that material power can solve problems that call for an altogether different approach. We might regard as an instance the attitude of Austria in 1914, that it must assert its power to tame the spirit of Serbia, disregarding the danger that such action could trigger a far greater conflict. A not dissimilar miscalculation has frequently been made in our own times by those colonial powers which in the face of insurgent nationalisms have believed the medicine of force would cure the rebelliousness of their colonial subjects, as the Portuguese still do in Angola and the South Africans with respect to the colored peoples in the midst of which they live. Such powers are preparing for themselves a continuity of deepening problems that cannot cease until they radically change their policies. For the Union of South Africa it is a particularly difficult and dangerous problem, that of an entrenched powerholding minority encompassed by a many-group disprivileged, disfranchised, and alien majority. But the handwriting on the wall is clear.

May we not regard the situation of our Southern whites as another case of vain reliance on superior power? Since desegregation is the law of the land, the strong and bitter resistance to it rests on nothing now but the illicit resort to material power, the economic and political controls still exercised by officeholding whites. Finally, we must not omit from the count the special form of the subjection of subject peoples that has been made a fine art under the Soviet system, proclaiming the "true freedom" of these peoples, the freedom of puppet governments under the shelter of Soviet tanks.

Serious as are the consequences of the misunderstanding and the misdealings of the powerful in their relations with weaker peoples, they are less inherently perilous than the misunderstandings of great powers with one another. The exhibits of Part One told the catastrophic story of such misunderstandings and consequent miscalculations in the past half-century. A common miscalculation has been that of a prospective enemy's capacity for resistance against what is initially a superiority of armed might. This error has brought about the downfall of many aggressive potentates and peoples. A related miscalculation rests on the assumption—so easily fostered by the arrogance of power—that the leader who has won a succession of signal victories is therefore invincible, so that he proceeds to attack a fresh and formidable foe. This was the error that brought Napoleon and Hitler to ruin.

Success increases the natural aggressiveness of the man of power. He comes to believe in his star, his destiny, his inspired leadership. The spur of success to ambition has brought disaster on many men over every range of the power scale, from the general and the statesman to the petty officeholder. Cardinal Wolsey, the favorite statesman of Henry VIII, attributed to it his downfall, when, according to Shakespeare, he warned his aide, Cromwell:

> Cromwell, I charge thee, fling away ambition:
> By that sin fell the angels.

This warning, by the way, went unheeded by another Cardinal of much prominence, the unwary Cardinal Rohan, who to win favor at court allowed himself to become the victim of the famous "Queen's necklace" intrigue, which had some share in the outbreak of the French Revolution. But the list of those who fell by their inordinate ambition for power is lengthy.

We observe in passing that an undue belief in the efficacy of coercion is entertained not by the powerful alone. It is a common prejudice of the ignorant and the unthinking that forceful measures can solve the problems of society. They cherish a misplaced reliance on what the rod and the policeman's nightstick and drastic laws and heavy court sentences can do to suppress some ancient social evils. And too frequently they receive the support of the law itself. So they deal with the narcotics addict and the prostitute by putting them in prison. For many centuries it was held that cruel and brutal punishment was the best preventive of crime, in spite of continuous evidence that it did not succeed. Today there are those who clamor for harsh treatment as the cure for the increasing volume of juvenile delinquency. They do not seek to understand why under certain conditions, for certain groups in certain areas of our cities, the amount of delinquency is considerably higher than for other groups under other conditions. A similar attitude has found abundant expression in the attempt, peculiarly characteristic of our people, to suppress communistic tendencies by jailing, depriving of their jobs, or otherwise harassing the relatively small group who either remain, or were sometime in the past, followers of the Party line. Already in the seventeenth century, the famous satirist, Samuel Butler, had stated one good argument against this approach:

> He that complies against his will
> Is of his own opinion still.

Another reason is that the urge to suppress, given enough license, goes beyond the limits of its ostensible objective. So in the heyday of McCarthyism the inquisitors were not content with the un-earthing of a few Communists but reached after persons who had "leftist" ideas about economics or politics, not only Socialists and radicals but Keynesians, advocates of equal rights for Negroes, and so forth—a tendency by no means yet extinct.

Coercive power, given an inch, always wants an ell. The hunger for more of the man of might ends only in death. Other appetites become jaded or outworn, but not this one. The ageing statesman does not willingly relinquish his position. Adenauer of-fered to withdraw from the headship but quickly retracted the offer. De Gaulle, who obtained quasi-dictatorial power mainly owing to the Algerian impasse, might well have resigned when he had accomplished his task. With great statesmanship he had achieved the basis for a lasting peace to end a hopeless war. Had he thereafter resigned, like another Cincinnatus, his greatness and his fame would have been untarnished, rounded off in triumph. Many other great men, including several generals who also be-came statesmen—but not so successfully as De Gaulle—have fol-lowed the lure of power too far and too long, to their own sorrow and the detriment of their fame. Legend has it that Alexander the Great wept because he had no more worlds to conquer. It makes a good commentary on the insatiate appetite of power, but it is bad history. Alexander's last campaign, as he returned across the desert toward Babylon, ended in a great loss of his troops, and he died while striving to reorganize his dominions and planning new exploits of empire.

The realism and the arrogance of power constituted a favorite theme of Greek mythology and later of the great dramas of Greece. The Greeks had a special name for it, *hybris*. It was the central motive of the first and most marvelous of epics, the *Iliad* of the unknown Homer, which told of the wrath of Achilles and its great train of consequences, arising in the first place from the manner in which the leader of the Greek host, Agamemnon, insulted the great warrior by depriving him of his rightful booty. Many of the great dramas of Greece played on the same theme, the abuse of power, as, for example, the *Agamemnon* of Aeschylus, the *Antigone* of Sophocles, and the *Medea* of Euripides. Shakespeare took up the same theme in various plays, including his three greatest, *Hamlet, King Lear,* and *Macbeth,* and it has been reiterated in many a novel and play up to our own times.

We may conjecture that the root of the miscalculating rashness so often associated with exalted power is a loss of the sense of proportion. This conclusion has been implicit in our whole discussion of the subject. We have already adduced some reasons why high or supreme power over men tends to pervert the sense of proportion, and various other considerations support this view. The powerful are protected in a measure from the penalties their lesser miscalculations would have brought on ordinary mortals. If a scheme they promote goes awry, the harmful consequences are likely to fall on others. The failure can be attributed to the agents who did the great man's bidding. "The king can do no wrong" is a maxim that has only legal significance, but actual monarchs may become convinced that it is true in the literal sense. The lessons of experience are thus less easily learned by the mighty. After his most ghastly errors in the Second World War, Hitler believed the resulting disasters were all the fault of his generals, such able men as Halder and Paulus and Rommel, and even his most valiant troops he berated as cowards.

The possession of power magnifies the ego-weight in the scale of human values. Supreme power comes to spell supreme right-ness, the approach to infallibility. The man of might is surrounded by many who fear to question his decisions and by many who flatter him and applaud his wisdom. He is thus likely to view issues in a false perspective, and becomes particularly exposed to certain kinds of error, the error of pursuing his advantage beyond reasonable limits, of tempting fate by needless adventures, the error of underrating the resistance his action may arouse, and the error of refusing to make desirable concessions.

We have been thinking so far mainly of the ruler whose power is nearly untrammeled, the emperor, the monarch, the dictator. But on any level the power to command, where it is relatively free from direct control, is exposed to the same dangers. It is so whether the powerholder is an economic magnate or the director of a great philanthropic organization, the commander of a war-ship or the warden of a prison. Even where power is made re-sponsible, so that it can be held to account for its actions, it is often free to make its own decisions in the first instance and may find ways of avoiding the later accounting. We speak of democ-racy as "responsible government," but in democracies executive decisions of the highest moment must be taken on the initiative of the head of the state, in consultation with a small group of in-siders, and this is freedom enough to foster the characteristic temptations of power. An illustration is the action of the British and French governments when in 1959 they gave orders to their military forces to swoop down on Suez. Everywhere high power within its range of its uninhibited discretion is subject to the de-velopment of attitudes unfavorable to that sense of proportion which is so large a part of wisdom. In the political arena effective responsibility is attainable only in degree, and then only where a people is sufficiently alert and well-informed to bring the constant impact of public opinion to bear on the policies of its government.

Whatever the checks may be that are designed to make the powerful responsible, there is one type of situation in which these checks are hardest to apply, while it is also one that peculiarly calls for wise judgment. This is the time of crisis or grave national disturbance. It is a situation that demands quick and firm decisions. It is hard to be clearheaded in the midst of turmoil. Tempers are frayed and there are shrill cries for extremist measures. In such a situation the relative wisdom of alternative policies is likely to receive scant consideration. The aggressive leader who makes the loudest promises and advocates the most drastic action comes to the top, and crisis is likely to be followed by a new domination. Sheer forcefulness makes its strongest appeal in an atmosphere of grave uncertainty, anxiety, and insecurity. One of many illustrations of this type of situation is offered by the plight of the provincial revolutionary government of Kerensky. The Russian people were utterly disgruntled with the war; they ached for peace and they wanted land, land of their own. Kerensky was out for far-reaching reforms, but he was unwilling to beg for peace from Germany. This was the opportunity of the Bolsheviks. They offered an immediate peace, and they falsely promised their land to the peasants. Against the aggressiveness and extremism of the Bolsheviks, the Kerensky government succumbed. Thus the crisis ended in a formidable new domination, but one of a kind that, whatever its achievements in other directions, has kept the whole world in a state of most dangerous and costly tension ever since.

To sum up, while enterprise involves risk and policy can never prove its validity until after the test, the high enterprises of the powerful have so often ended in disaster that we have assumed, with some historical evidence, that great power is specially liable to grave error. Even if this assumption were disputed, it would still be important to examine the conditions attendant on high power that may be prejudicial to the success of its policies.

In this discussion we have implicitly limited our conclusion to a particular category of the powerful, those who are in love with power and consequently eager to increase their own. Human nature is variant for those who wear the crown no less than for men in every other rank of life. There have been kings and emperors and great statesmen who were mostly concerned with the constructive development of their domains or with the direct welfare of their peoples or with particular interests of their own, intellectual, social, or other. Augustus Caesar, once he had ended civil war and brought unity to his people, was mostly engaged in the restoration and rebuilding of his city and his land. He boasted he had found Rome brick and left it marble. A later emperor, Marcus Aurelius, who successfully defended Rome against barbarian attacks, was devoted to Stoicism and contemplation. James I of England, albeit a bit of a pedant, preferred peace to war, liked to write books, and sponsored the Authorized Version of the Bible. Other rulers have been too much preoccupied with their pleasures, with "women, wine, and song," to be concerned with the furtherance of their power. It is noteworthy, in passing, that potentates who have been pleasure lovers, while they may have corrupted individuals and lowered public morale by their licentious courts, have been less dangerous to the general welfare of their peoples than the aggressive power lovers who have wrought such havoc on their own country as well as on the countries they attacked. Perhaps the most deadly of all autocrats have been the ascetic ones in whom all other interests were overmastered by their engrossment in the pursuit of power, whether they sought it merely for their own aggrandizement or claimed to be vindicating the greatness of their peoples or, in the insolence of their folly, to be promoting the true faith and the glory of God.

The men who come from below and fight their way to the headship, being lovers of power from the first, are likely to be the most aggressive of leaders, and overaggressiveness is the most dangerous of human attributes. But the temptations of the possession of power are such that many of those to whom power came as the gift of birth or the accident of fortune have also yielded to them. The possession of great power is prejudicial to the more kindly and humane of human qualities. Among its other characteristics it appears to be usually fatal to the capacity for humor, which itself is a manifestation of the sense of proportion. We can hardly conceive of a capacity for humor in a Hitler or, say, a Torquemada.

Because of the uncontrolled aggressiveness of the men of might, many stretches of human history have resembled, in the famous words put by Shakespeare into the mouths of a king whose lust for power led him to his own destruction,

> . . . a tale
> Told by an idiot, full of sound and fury,
> Signifying nothing.

14.

Conspectus

Behind the endless vicissitudes and commotions of recorded history, behind the endless ravishings and oppressions of human beings that leave no memory, out of the perpetual drive for power that is innate in human beings and human groups, social trends of great persistence have worked and emerged. The expansion of society beyond the larger family, the tribe, gave a new significance to the leadership, the ruling group, now armed with greater material resources. The hunger for domination had new opportunities. The powerholders jealously guarded their power against the powerless, enshrined it in myths, clothed it with an aura of authority to tame the minds of their subjects so as to turn them into instruments in the drive for greater power. In the consequent wars of the powerful, the victors built up principalities and empires that sometimes endured through centuries, until new victors rose to overthrow them.

Such was the pattern of affairs over the greater portion of recorded history. Significant changes were, however, immanent and brewing from early times. The mass instrument of power, manpower itself, was made of the same stuff as the masters who used it. For all their precautions, the masters were not always able to prevent their instrument from turning against them. The peoples murmured among themselves—echoes of such murmurs occasionally are heard in the aristocratic literature of the ancient world, for all recorded literature of these times was aristocratic, since the only patrons and readers were the elite or those associated with them. In Homer's *Iliad* there is a member of the Greek host, Thersites, who impudently criticizes his betters and gets mocked and buffeted for his pains, an ugly fellow who doesn't know his place. It is only in the more democratic Athens of the fifth century that we find any literature of protest against the exactions of the aristocracy. There were times, however, when the subject masses were rendered so exacerbated and desperate because of the impositions of the landowners that they rose in revolt, but nearly always the masters, being organized and equipped, were able to subdue any resistance. The mere rebellion of the hungry, the ignorant, and the dispossessed was unavailing so long as the dogmas of authority and the magic of power controlled the minds of the folk.

Every established elite must cultivate the magic of power. It may magnify its service but it must magnify its role, its status, its authority. The mere panoply of power is itself impressive, and it is thus all the easier to invest that power with a quality in the powerful not possessed by ordinary men. The elite have the mission to rule. It is predestinated, sanctioned by heaven, divinely appointed. Under the *ancien régime* men obeyed, not because they understood why the command was given or what purpose it served, but because their minds were attuned to obedience. The ruler did not need to justify his command. There was a magic in his authority to compel obedience.

Even from the earliest historical times, there were ethical and religious prescriptions that in some degree and under favorable conditions tended to mitigate the arbitrariness of rule. But the evidence of history is plain to the effect that no proclamation of ethical and religious doctrines, however exalted or however sacrosanct, can protect a people from the devastating ambitions of power unless such doctrines are embodied in political institutions guarded by the vigilance of a sovereign people. The doctrines themselves are highly significant of the deeper promptings of the nature of men, and they endure, in some form, through the ages, finding some manner of vindication in the secular trends to which we shall presently return.

In the fourth and third centuries B.C. a series of remarkable civilizations developed in the Mesopotamian area and the lands of the Southeastern Mediterranean. The first great example was the Babylonian Empire, based on a chain of important cities. It was followed by the Assyrian Empire after a time of flux. Egypt developed another distinctive civilization, and the smallest territory of these lands, Judea, was destined to play the greatest of historical roles. All these peoples had religions that, unlike the religions of the classical period, were woven into the fabric of society. The ethical principles they proclaimed laid stress on justice and fair dealing. Thus they offered a degree of protection to the common people, certain rights of redress against gross violations of the code. The recognition of such rights varied with changing rulers and their officials. They were wholly insecure, often at the mercy of the rapacity of the tax collector, the military recruiter, or the local headman, and in the frequent hostilities between peoples they were of no avail. It was much the same in the great empire of China, where religion was primarily ethical and not theological. Here the people were extremely poor and suffered even more from disastrous droughts and other calamities. The great teachers, beginning with Lao-tse in the sixth century B.C., were held in high respect, but their doctrines were no guarantee against manifold abuses, and there were long periods when in this loose-jointed empire the strife between powerholders and powerseekers despoiled the land. The chief protection left to the people was the strong familial ties that remained nearly intact through it all.

In Judea, a high religious culture was shared by the people as a whole, so that their prophets were in some ways more potent than their kings. Their prophets and their priests were the lawmakers, and the sacred Law was above the ruler, and, since it laid down quite specific codes of justice and "righteousness," going into elaborate procedural details, the people possessed some assurance of rights other peoples lacked. The theocratic structure, however, was less favorable to the development of political than of civil rights, rights before the law. The main line of political development went instead through Greece, where the "demagication" of rulership was of a wholly revolutionary character. The weakness was that, partly because of its slave basis, Greek civilization provided no clear principle on which a popular government could be established. There is indeed no substitute for the magic of superimposed authority except the cohesive will of the people. But Greece gave the world the first example of a structured democracy, though its citizenship was severely restricted and the experiment itself was short-lived. Nowhere else on earth is there any evidence that such a political credo as the Funeral Speech of Pericles had ever been uttered before.

The magic of power prevailed, sometimes needing the help of tyranny, and found new forms of embodiment. But a breach had been made. Two new concepts, antagonistic to the old order, had been proclaimed. One was that ruling power should be functional, not arbitrary but limited to the fulfillment of its proper function, the well-being of the citizens. The other was that ruling power should be bestowed by the people, to be subject to their will and transferred by them when they so decided by their electoral votes. A very significant aspect of considerably later history was the struggle, confused and fluctuating as it was, to bring these principles nearer to realization. It is a struggle that still goes on, for in this field no victory is ever complete, but in the process vast transformations have occurred.

Every conferment of rights, civil or political, on an originally subject class narrows the distance between rulers and ruled and involves a change not only in the distribution but also in the character of power. The investment of a subject class with rights is a conferment of a degree of power on them, the power to pursue new opportunities, to seek new objectives, to give expression to their opinions. It is social power, with a degree of economic power, and an approach to political power. So long as the magic of rulership was dominant—the aura of sovereignty, the "divinity [that] doth hedge a king"—it meant a compulsion not only of the body but also of the mind. Now these other forms of power began to exist independently, or rather in their own right, until when the process was sufficiently advanced they challenged the primal power and made it subservient to themselves. This consummation is reached so far as government rests on consensus.

We have endeavored to trace the slow, deep-working, stubbornly resisted trends that at length brought many peoples within reach of this consummation. They include the following: the admission of certain rights and liberties to appease the discontent or the rebelliousness of subject peoples; the first brief flowering of a limited democracy in Athens and again in Rome, setting an example and enunciating a principle that had some sporadic influence until the times were ripe for its fuller development; the ending of all absolute monarchies, usually through the gradual wresting of rights by the more privileged classes and then in turn by the under classes; the abolition over practically all the earth of the once widespread system of slavery; the nearly total erosion of the colonial empire, in quite recent times extending over the greater part of the earth; the spread of education to the masses, a process that in many backward areas is only now gaining momentum; and the political emancipation of women, the most recent of all these trends to make great strides.

Taken all together, the advance of these processes has meant an inclusive liberation, not only of the common people from the subjection they once endured, but at the same time of the other forms of power, cultural, social, economic, civil, and political, that at an earlier stage were the mere appanages of the primary power of physical coercion. Such liberation is of course by no means complete, its extent varying greatly in different countries.

In passing, we might note that the process of liberation was aided considerably by the unwisdom of the powerholders themselves. Under most conditions the mass of human beings are patiently submissive to the arbitrary demands of their rulers, being receptive to the indoctrinations that teach them their lowly place and glorify the men of might. But power, being easily blinded to its own limits, is not unlikely to become overbearing, contemptuous of the inferior, ruthless in its demands. Thus it breaks through the resistance point, and the murmurings of the people swell to tumults, uprisings, revolts. The disorder may go so far that some new strong man may find the opportunity to seize control. If the disturbance goes deep enough, it may be a man of the people, and then the hallowed system is severely shaken. Or again the aggressive ruler may engage in rash military adventures, coveting greater power and prating of glory, only to end in disaster. But the follies of overweening power are many, and our own age has presented remarkable exhibits of them, which we have endeavored to depict in Part One of this book.

The manner in which the liberation of these social forms of power from the handcuffs of arbitrary rulership has changed the character of society would constitute a major theme in the social history of mankind. It may suffice to reiterate that free cultural power, in all its manifestations, artistic, literary, philosophical, and religious, is creative in a very special sense. Its products are modes of communication, that have the potentiality of enduring practically intact through time. They are new and unique, unlike anything that is purely physical, expressions of what never was before on sea or land, entering under the sifting assessment of the generations into the lengthening heritage of universal man.

All forms of power, even the most creative, can be constructive or destructive after their kind. All forms of power, even the most remote from the physical, exercise some measure of compulsion on men, leading them, influencing them, persuading them, setting them an example, inducing them to some form of action. The political form, whether directly or through the sanction it gives to other organizations, alone has the right of physical compulsion, when its authority is flouted or its laws violated. The compulsion exerted by other organizations is a compulsion over the will, not over the body. It ranges from mild influence to the spell of revered authority, from acquiescence for the sake of patronage or hoped-for favors to the sheer subservience of the needy to the demands of those on whom their livelihood depends. Economic power is a particularly effective source of control; with its free command over goods and services, dispensing jobs and giving out contracts, owning the means to advance its own interest directly and through its own organs of communication, it has an impact on society that is very persuasive. When economic power is great and concentrated, its influence permeates nearly every area of social activity.

Power always tells, no matter what its form. The control it exercises depends on its kind and scale, on the personality of its possessor, on the strategy of which he is capable, on the character of the situation. While power has become mainly functional, the power of the appointed officeholder, it always has its area of discretion, its degree of autonomy, its latitude of interpretation of its commission, and therefore the opportunity to act in an arbitrary manner within these limits, regardless of the responsibility attached to its function. As we have pointed out, the arbitrary employment of power is particularly notable in the political arena.

Power always creates grades, rankings, distinctions. It is so in the most "egalitarian" society as well as in the aristocratic type. We have dwelt on the increasingly widespread distribution of power and the correspondingly greater range of liberties and opportunities that historical trends have developed over large areas of society. But that change does not mean that elites have ceased to flourish. The decaying Soviet ideology envisioned a future in which the state and all the apparatus of social as well as political power would be abolished, but the "transitional" stage that was presumed to prepare the way for this ideal system is fully as elite-dominated as any other society in the whole historical record. What the historical transformation did was to undermine the foundations of corporate elites determined by birth or prior status, so that instead elites rest largely on function or achievement or popular appraisal of some kind, with a diminishing carry-over of status, usually buttressed by inherited wealth, to the near descendants of those who had won elite standing.

In our many-peaked, functionally oriented society, the distribution of power is exceedingly complex and peculiarly unstable. The formal allocation of power is no index of the actual residence of power. There are several reasons why it is so. Sometimes the nominal headship is an honorific appointment, whether because of the prestige of a name or as a reward for previous service, while the effective control is in the hands of other officials. Sometimes a headman is "kicked upstairs" to some honorific position as a way of removing him from the real headship. Sometimes the governing board of an organization, its legal authority, is in effect a rubber stamp for a decisive president or other top executive. Again, the power any individual or any organization wields is relative in many situations to his or its relationship to other power units. An organization plans its policies not only in competition with other organizations but usually also in concert with some other organizations. The businessman constantly makes deals with some of his competitors, openly or covertly, with respect to output, pricing, marketing, and so forth. His success depends on his strategy. The politician does the same thing in his own distinctive way. In union is power, up to a point. Counterdeals by an opposing concert of powers have to be met. Agreements between powerholders are superseded, and new combinations are always being formed. Chance and circumstance, technological change, changes in consumer attitudes, fashion changes, external factors of various kinds play the role of fate or fortune. Leadership passes into new hands, as older leaders weaken or miscalculate or fall behind the times. Power is in ferment in the small circle and in the great state, and the consequences in any area have repercussions within many others.

Let us by way of illustration look at the power structure of a particular town of moderate size. If we ask who are its leaders we have first some obvious candidates—the mayor, the somewhat aggressive owner of the big milling plant that is the town's main industry, also a member of the town's oldest and most respected family who is the very active chairman of several civic organizations, and a successful lawyer who has political ambitions. Beyond these there is a popular town councillor who is prominent in various social clubs, a banker who belongs to a well-established family of the region, and a lady of means, a youngish widow, who is the style leader, a supporter of various worthy causes, and a prominent and uncompromising member of the dominant political party. These are the chief "personages" of the community, but there are also power factors operating less through personalities than through collectivities. The town has a considerable Italian population and a smaller Irish one, and on some issues they join forces, usually under some understanding with the common church to which they adhere. On the other side, there is a fairly vocal but much-less-coherent Protestant group, which, however, has the advantage of representing the older-established social class of the town. More recently, a trade-union organizer who represents the mill operatives has become a troublemaker in the eyes of the elite—which means he has also become somewhat of a power.

Within this complex can we say that any personality or group of personalities, any organization or coalition of organizations is dominant? It is true that one political party has been in the ascendant and can usually be counted on to win the elections, though not with the large majorities of early days. But the party

itself must cater to local interests, much as the opposition party would do if it came to power. And there are strong minority interests, ethnic or religious, "real estate" or "reform," which on occasion can muster a compact front against policies of the party in power and deter it from taking action on them.

As for purely local politics, the mayor and his council majority are relatively unimportant in decisionmaking. On substantial issues they decide in accord with the wishes of their most influential supporters, and on matters of patronage, which are usually their major concern, they are subservient to a gentleman who hardly ever figures in the news, the boss of the party machine. A minority member of the council, an able spokesman, has led, with occasional success, an attack on the doings and deals of the council. In at least one instance the chairman of the school board, a man highly respected but usually inactive in politics, organized a vigorous campaign for a reform of the school system involving an increased budget, and won out against much official opposition. The well-known "personages" of the community have rarely, if ever, shown this type of effective leadership, being in general moderately influential supporters of the "establishment."

The group which is generally regarded as the elite, having as its rather small core the more prominent members of the old-established well-to-do families, with a number of business heads and some leading professionals as its outer circle, is rather less influential than it was a generation or two ago. It cannot be said to be decisive in community affairs. The alignment of opposing sides changes as issues change. And that process has been quickened in the last decade, as new arrivals have settled in the town and two relatively small but growing new businesses have been introduced. New problems come with new conditions, new leaders supersede old ones. Even if we could fully assess the power structure as of a particular date, it would in all probability undergo some significant change within a few years.

Whatever the scale of community, the village or town or great city or region or country, there lies behind all determination of policy, behind all important decisions of executive power, the crisscross of organized interests, the push and pull of groupings each concerned for its own dominance, the strong or weak strategy of opposing leaders. The pattern is universal, but in each case the configuration is variant. Besides the more specific factors we have mentioned, any assessment would need to take into account the character and level of public concern, the areas of considerable public indifference, and the role played by the popular media of communication.

There is, however, one type of situation in which, no matter what the alignment of forces, decisive action reverts into the hands of a single leader, whether the official head of the organization or some powerholder at his back. It might happen on any organizational level, but the salient instances come from the highest. It is a necessity of the crisis situation, where a grave decision must be made forthwith, at the heart of the crisis. The wrong alternative will spell disaster, the right alternative—right because it succeeds—will rescue the situation. This was the kind of decision President Kennedy had to make after the discovery of the Soviet long-range missiles set up in Cuba. The sole responsibility, with its immense hazards, was his, no matter what his advisers might say. De Gaulle played a similar role in two times of crisis, after the fall of France and again in the political impasse when France was strained and weakened by the weary Algerian War, while the extreme right in France was fomenting insurrection. Often enough, in the troubled history of our times, some leader has been called on to make a fateful choice between alternatives.

He may be misguided, he may fail in any event, and disaster may follow—such is the nature of the crucial decision.

We have been dwelling mainly on the policymaking process, but we would have a quite inadequate idea of the role of social power if we thought of it only in its policymaking role. Much of the time it is engaged in manipulations, in quiet deals for its own advantage, in stratagems and reprisals, as well as in a multitude of routine affairs. It is in such activities that functional power has the best opportunity and the strongest temptation to become arbitrary. There are jealousies and rancors that deflect its energies and create divisions between near-equals in the echelons of power. There are impositions of the upper on the lower, with undue advantage taken of place and status, the disparagement of meritorious service that does not cater to the whims and foibles of superiors, schemes to secure undeserved awards, scandalmongering and chicanery, false assumptions of credit for the work of underlings. The devoted administrator will rise above the grosser of these failings, but in greater or lesser degree they are to be found beneath the placid surface of large-scale organizations.

In spite of the persistence of arbitrary power within functional organizations, the secular transformation of authority has greatly limited its role. Within the more democratic societies of the modern world, arbitrary power no longer exists of right but mostly in the interstices of functional power, an abuse of authority subject to some measure of control. The change is of the highest significance.

The most important difference is the widened opportunity for the evocation of human potentialities. When people are free from arbitrary arrest and condemnation, they cease to regard authority as a tyrannous master. When the government is their own, they can express their opinions openly, criticize it at will, dismiss it from office when the majority are discontented with it. When people can vote freely, they become for the first time citizens in any real sense of the term. When they have access to education, when their ability is no longer numbed and fettered by class barriers, their qualities of mind and heart, whatever they may be, have a chance of development and expression they lacked before. When a people is no longer under the rule of an external power, no matter if it is in degree benevolent, they gain a sense of belongingness, of being at home on their own good earth, though they may still be in some danger of falling under the domination of some power-hungry clique among themselves.

Wherever the opportunities for the evocation of personality are thus expanded, more ways of life are opened up, more directions are explored by more people, more advances along many lines are made possible. It was in certain areas of enlarged opportunity, as in Athens, in Rome, in Florence, in Elizabethan England, that the greater cultural advances of mankind have been achieved, to become part of the heritage of the race. The taming of arbitrary power by no means assures such advances, but only when some liberation from it prevails is it likely to happen at all.

We cannot predict that the trend of liberation from arbitrary power will continue. In some periods it has been slow, in some quickened, and in some it has suffered severe reversals. In our own days the spread of Communism has been pernicious to the fundamental freedom, the freedom of the mind. Nevertheless in its homeland the Communist regime has gone far to abolish the illiteracy and the total resourcelessness that were characteristic of the previous serfdom, and this development itself may yet be of real importance in enabling the people to win through to the liberty of opinion. There are already certain indications that might be interpreted as favoring such a conclusion.

Finally, there are two prospective developments that, should they be fulfilled, would be likely to sustain the continuance of the secular trend. One is the advancement of the mass of humanity from the precarious subsistence level at which over the larger portion of the earth they have remained through all the ages up to the present time. For those who are resourceless and opportunityless, the other freedoms are of scant avail. The slavery of abject need makes a mockery of the "rights of man." They can be neither won nor maintained under that condition. But already the technology of production has reached the point where it could be applied for the gradual raising of the subsistence level everywhere. The obstacles to this achievement lie no longer in the "niggardliness of nature" but only in the unwisdom of men. Assuming that the necessary amount of technical and financial aid is provided by the wealthier nations, the remaining obstacles are the traditions engendered under the old order that took for granted the poverty of the masses and the domination of small elites which profited from their powerlessness; the problem of modifying the ways of life congenial to these conditions, confirmed as they are by the inertia and ignorance of the many and by the self-interest of the few; the danger of destroying the morale of the people wedded to old ways of living; and beyond all that the resistance to the necessary birth-control measures without which the inevitable increase of population, with the introduction of modern hygiene and of a more productive economy, would defeat the growth of prosperity. These obstacles are not insuperable—the more advanced countries, and quite recently Japan, have in great measure overcome not dissimilar obstacles, but in the earlier stages only slow progress seems likely.

The other portent is the menace and the promise of the harnessing of atomic energy. If sanity prevails, it will mean the end of great international wars. The know-how of the hydrogen bomb, and possibly of even more appalling types, can never be obliterated, and therefore no nation which possessed it could trust any agreement with other possessors committing them to abjure nuclear arms and revert to what is euphemistically called "conventional" warfare. If the era of major wars were ended, it would mean that the climactic form of physical coercion, the violence loosed by the great state, would cease to be a controlling factor in international affairs. Just as the taming of physical coercion by arbitrary rule within the state has been a condition of the enlargement of the rights and liberties of the many, so this greatest renunciation of violence as an instrument of policy would mean a new reign of law across the earth, might have some effect in limiting tendencies of the much-engrossing state to usurp excessive controls, and would make possible the conversion of enormous sums, now devoted to military defense, to the development of the vast potential of service for social, educational, and cultural well-being, and thus give a new impetus to the constructive processes of society.

Commentary

SOME FOLLOW-UP CONSIDERATIONS ON
TOPICS TREATED IN THE TEXT

The Responsibility for the First World War (pages 11–14)

In Chapter 1 I have taken the position that, as Sidney Brad-shaw Fay put it in his work, *The Origins of the World War,* "none of the Powers wanted a European War." This judgment is far from being universally accepted, and the partisans of each side still blame it on the other. History offers us no Q.E.D.s. I have tried to read the complicated evidences as impartially as I could. While some of the powers did much less to prevent war than others, being preoccupied with their immediate nationalistic objectives, none showed enough foresighted statesmanship directed to preventing the catastrophe. Once certain initial blunders were made, they triggered a sequence of actions that led with a kind of fatal automatism to the European War. Once Austria and

Serbia became thoroughly embroiled, the militarist elements in Germany and Russia and Austria came more and more into control in the absence of potent leadership. Secret commitments and open alliances divided Europe, making it impossible to localize the conflict. Public opinion in the various countries, though still dominantly averse from war, was excited and then inflamed by the nationalist press. Back of the embroilment lay a long tangled story of intrigues, nationalist jealousies, and the ambitions and aggressions of the men of power, ending with the fateful folly of Archduke Francis Ferdinand in visiting Sarajevo on its day of national mourning for an ancient defeat and enslavement; but it was the reckless demands of Austria and the intransigence of the Serbs that precipitated the disaster. The rest was the bankruptcy of diplomacy.

The Might-Have-Beens of History (pages 20–22)

The world of action is a world of contingencies. In our everyday affairs an important change of direction may depend on what seems the merest chance, on a casual meeting, on a sheer accident, if we think of the statistical odds against its happening. On the same reckoning it is the grossest improbability that any particular individual was ever born. Such contingencies seem not infrequently to determine the great turning points of history. *If* the German authorities hadn't contrived to give Lenin passage through to Russia in 1917, *if* a certain plot against Hitler that nearly succeeded had actually succeeded—and so on—how different the course of events might have been! "A grain of sand in a man's flesh," said Napoleon, may mean the fall of an empire.

And have we not all heard the ditty about the missing horseshoe nail?

It would be rash to assert that if something had not happened, if, say, some momentous decision had not been made, some other specified occurrence would have taken place. We cannot reckon with the contingencies that would have operated in the absence of any particular event. But it would not be unreasonable to presume that had the momentous decision not been made, certain direct consequences of that decision would not have occurred. Such negative might-have-beens, the would-not-have-beens, are much less precarious than the positive ones. It is, for example, not unreasonable to believe that had the peace of Versailles been constructive instead of punitive and rapacious, Hitler would not have had the opportunity to rise to power in Germany. The conclusion is still speculative but certainly within the range of probability.

While historical events are the play of contingency, the greater historical trends or movements have deeper roots. They depend on no man's edict nor on any group's policies. They are tides that swell and ebb responsive to the dominant urges or demands of human nature as they find vent under the changing conditions. Such is the nature of the major systems of thought and culture, of longer-term developments in the arts, sciences, and technologies. These are the genuine historymakers, if we view history in a broad enough perspective.

Characterization of the "Spineless Years" (pages 27–42)

To characterize any period as exhibiting a particular attitude or quality is at best a retrospective summation of a tendency that has particular significance because of the impact it had on the times and the legacy it left the times to come. During such a period people generally are unaware of its character. Over the period here referred to few indeed thought of it as exhibiting, in its leadership and in its public responsiveness to conditions, a failure of nerve, a lack of will to understand and cope with impending perils. But may we not rightly so characterize a time in which the United States retired into a parochial insulation, renouncing the call to leadership, in which thoughtless speculation and stupid tariff-making paralyzed the economic reconstruction so urgently needed in the afterwar years, in which statesmanship in Europe was at its lowest ebb, when security was sought by despoiling the former enemies and annexing parts of their territory, when the unity that had sustained the Allies during the war was squandered in nationalistic jealousies, when industrialists and politicians looked approvingly on the braggadocio Mussolini because he "put the Communists where they belonged" and was supposed to make the Italian railroads run on time, when the League of Nations lacked the will to make its economic blockade effective after Mussolini had wantonly attacked Ethiopia, and when even the obvious menace of Hitler failed to impress the then dominant powers—until it was too late. It falls within the tragic irony of history that after a time of ceaseless tension and heroic sacrifice, when release comes at length, the yearning for ease and gratification takes precedence over the urgent need to meet the insistent problems of resettlement—until again it is too late.

Physical Energy and Human Power (pages 75–76)

In the text we have subsumed under the one category of power both physical energies and the means human beings employ (and to a lesser extent other organic creatures) in the business of living. But the difference between the two is so great that it may be a stretch of language to include them within any one category. We say, for example, certain rays have the power to injure or kill us. So has a gun in a man's hand. The gun is instrumental. Its power is its threat or its use. All human powers are mediated by an internal organic system of controls, usually involving an overt design. The ray is not instrumental. Its power is its being. It *is* an energy. The whole physical world is energy, eternally following the law of its being. Man uses this energy *in order* to make it serve certain purposes, to satisfy certain needs. It is human power *as thus applied*.

Functional and Nonfunctional Power (page 82)

The dichotomy we have drawn between *functional* power and *free* power may need some further clarification. The primary distinction is between power that is specifically assigned or entrusted or at the least assented to for the performance of a particular function, which may be very broad in its scope or narrowly limited. It is characteristic of every kind of modern organization. Consequently the *arbitrary* employment of power means the abuse of functional power to serve the interests of the powerholder in ways that are inconsistent with or prejudicial to the function assigned to the organizational executive.

Free power on the other hand signifies power to act in ways that are not limited by assigned function or prohibited by legal regulation. Hobbes defined freedom as the area over which the laws are silent. It was not a good definition of freedom—since some laws protect the citizen from molestation and thus enlarge his area of freedom—but we may say that free power is the power to act outside the limits of legal obligation or functional prescription. In spite of the multiplicity of laws, there are numerous situations in which the citizen is free to choose at will what he desires to do. The man of prestige has a wider range of free power, since his lead and his influence win respect. So has the man of wealth. The greatest amplitude of free power is that of the absolute ruler who rules either as a kind of divinity, not seriously bound by any constitution, or else by sheer force of arms. Outside of democracy all rulers have a considerable but varying range of unregulated or free power.

The term *arbitrary* has less direct significance for the exercise of free power than for that of functional power. Free power may be tyrannical or overbearing or brutal or immoral without being illegitimate. But in a looser sense we may call the exercise of free power arbitrary when it exhibits the mere caprice or wantonness of the ruler.

Liberty Under Democracy and Under Dictatorship (pages 94–95)

The distinction between the power structures of dictatorship and of democracy, as developed in the text, is applicable only to the extent in which dictatorships and democracies exemplify the principles on which they are respectively founded. Stalin's dictatorship was a genuine example, whereas under Khrushchev various modifications have developed. Caudillo rule in Latin America is dictatorship only in degree. Democracy on the other hand at best only approaches its professed objectives, and the term "democracy" is made to include forms of government that are a long way from the democratic goal. We must also remember that the primal liberty of democracy, the liberty so notably enunciated in the passage from Milton's *Areopagitica* quoted on page 94, does not depend solely on the form of government but also in significant measure on the temper of public opinion. Since the time of De Tocqueville there have been charges that American democracy, for all its presumed individualistic tendencies, has been strongly conformist, manifesting intolerance against outgroups.

Power, Liberty, and Right (pages 94–96)

In the same context we may distinguish three closely inter-related terms. The power to do anything, when it is legal or free power, is also the liberty to do it. But the liberty to act is not necessarily the capacity to act. Any man is free to write a play, compose music, or build a home, but he may lack the qualifications or the interest or the means. Legal power is not actual power, but only a safeguard against outside interference should the actual power, the capacity, be present. A legal power is equivalently a right. It is power since it imposes an obligation on others not to encroach on your liberty in doing what it thus permits you to do. But everyone has rights that he is either unwilling or unable to exercise. Rights and obligations are reciprocal.

Scientific Knowledge and Popular Beliefs (pages 114–115)

It is a common misunderstanding that modern scientific knowledge is so complex, intricate, remote from ordinary conceptions, and expressed in such elaborate mathematical formulas as to be beyond the grasp of the average—or above average—man. It is certainly true that no human being, not even the greatest scientist, can compass more than a small fraction of the specific knowledge that hundreds of thousands of researchers in a thousand different fields are adding to the storehouse of learning. It is also true that in the primary areas of atomic physics and cosmic physics the processes of experimentation, calculation, and inference call for long training and high intelligence and are thus quite beyond the comprehension of the man in the street. But the great new understanding science has been offering us concerning the nature of the universe, the forces that work eternally in the inconceivably small particles that make up what we call matter, the laws that regulate the motions of the stars and galaxies and determine the processes of their becoming and being and ending, the way life has developed on this earth from the first replicating cell to the piece of work called man, the way human society has developed, responsive to the appetites, the passions, the needs, the insights, the experiences of that devious, unresting, still mysterious capacity, the mind of man—this new understanding science can surely convey far more adequately and far more widely than has yet been achieved.

In certain scientific circles a supercilious attitude is adopted toward the "popularizer," as if any such endeavor meant "writing down" for popular edification. It may also be that many scientists (being engrossed with the challenging problems of day-to-day research) are hardly aware themselves of the perspective of this knowledge. In any event some scientific leaders have combined fine perception with the power of communication—T. H. Huxley was a notable example, and in our own day several physicists have shown a similar capacity. The great success of Harlow Shapley's little book, *Of Stars and Men,* indicates the receptivity of the public. But our educational systems, for all their new emphasis on science, are extremely reluctant to expose their pupils to the new perspective of science and to its social implications.

Source of Form of Power (page 139)

The perceptive reader will have noticed that on various occasions we have referred to some property or condition or attribute as a "source or form" of power. We can say, for example, "knowledge is power," or "knowledge is a source of power." The two statements may be fully equivalent, but if we stress the word "source" we are thinking of knowledge as an intermediate condition in the attainment of an end. Knowledge, for example, is necessary to contrive a device that in turn can be applied to achieve some purpose. Knowledge, however, enables us to find our direction without resort to any intermediate device. In the last resort all the forms of power we refer to on whatever level, such as organization, armed might, professional ability, artistic skill, are in strict logic simply sources of power, made effective by the will to employ them, in other words, by the dominating drives, urges, purposes of human beings.

Can Organizations Exist in Their Own Right? (page 142)

Do organizations have value in themselves, apart from the service they render? We sometimes speak as though they did. We speak of the greatness, the magnificence, the grandeur of the state, as though it were something nobler or finer than the quality of its people. The devout, especially if they adhere to certain faiths, think of the Church as something holy in itself, in its own right, apart from the sanctity of its leaders or its members, as if it had an indwelling spirit, apart from the spirit that animates the behavior of its people. And there have been certain schools of philosophy, notably the Platonic and the Hegelian, which regarded the great collectivity, the state in particular, as something of supreme worth in itself. Hegel wrote that the state was "the march of God on earth," but he had little respect for the will of the people. In a grosser vein, Hitler spoke contemptuously of the German folk, but Germany, the embodiment of the master race, was ineffably great.

An organization certainly possesses attributes that are not possessed by its members severally or as a mere aggregate of persons. It has a power, an authority characterizing it as a system. It has a potential immortality. It has a history, a tradition all its own. It preserves and guards the great memorials of the past. Under its auspices enduring institutions are established, great enterprises undertaken, great services initiated and endowed.

The great organization may certainly deserve the regard and the admiration, as well as the allegiance, of its members. But its value is the value of what has been achieved through it and in its name, the value of what it stands for and what it advances. It is the value of its service to the commonweal. The view that it exists in its own right has been favored by the ruling class in class-bound societies, as well as by despots and absolute monarchs. For such the state did not exist to serve its people, and it was expedient to magnify the abstraction of the state, as a cloak for the class interests it served instead. The people were instructed that there was "a mystery in the soul of state." But a democratic state must stand on its service, present and past.

Let us consider the case where a state has manifestly been responsible for atrocious crimes, say Hitler's Germany. It was no abstraction that was guilty, it was Hitler and his gang, and the people who supported him. If we say it was the government and not the state, the distinction is here meaningless, for no state does anything except through its government and indirectly through the people who support its government. It is always people, leaders and followers, who achieve, for the state is their agency. It is always people who are guilty, as it is always people who suffer. The argument can be expressed in more sophisticated terms, but the conclusion would remain the same.

It is characteristic of certain historians and political theorists that they speak of states as though they were impersonal entities that coldly calculate and plan, always in terms of power. They have no other motivations, no other concerns. They have no goals except to gain more power and to defend themselves against other entities that have equally no other goals. For practical purposes the world is simply composed of these impersonal entities, greater or smaller, each engaged with its own self-centered power quest, uniting and dividing in order to strengthen themselves and to protect themselves from others. They have no interest in human beings, no interest in the thousand other concerns of humanity. This viewpoint is acclaimed as realism, political realism.

No doubt much of history, as usually recorded, is susceptible of interpretation in this manner. Rulers and councils of ministers spend a considerable portion of their energy and time in this sort of planning. But they are human beings, not power computers, and they have worries and passions and interests of many other kinds. Sometimes they are interested even in the welfare of their peoples. The people in turn are a very important part of the state. Without them there would be no state. Their interest in the state as power is usually secondary, often remote. The more they make their state their own the more unreal becomes the reality of the *real-politikers*.

The Significance of Certain Long-Term Trends in Human Relationships (pages 156–157)

Not enough attention has been paid to the manner in which a series of meaningfully consistent trends have, in spite of longer or shorter periods of retreat or apparent disappearance, developed and overrode opposing interests and traditions. In the text we have concentrated on four such trends, but these are simply major aspects of a many-sided process. If we compare the characteristic social system of the first great civilizations of recorded history, or even that of the earlier Middle Ages, with the great majority of present-day societies, the contrast in this respect is quite remarkable. Among the changes thus featured we include the following: the abolition of slavery; the near disappearance of serfdom; the obsolescence of monarchical government and the vast increase of republican states; the abolition or radical reduction of the exclusive prerogatives formerly attached to birth, prior status, and land-ownership; the rise of open competitive systems of social class; the establishment of practically universal suffrage in many lands; the collapse of empire and the rise to statehood of former colonial territories; the new tendency of the "have" countries to provide the "have-nots" with economic and technical aid; the reformation of old penal systems with their tortures and brutal punishments; the spread of social welfare programs to give some protection against unemployment, destitution, and the disabilities of the

aged; and the advance of the insurgent movement attacking economic and social discrimination against disprivileged groups and
especially colored groups.

We may find some partial explanation of this great transformation of social power in concomitant changes, the great increase
of productivity through technological advance and the development of industry, the consequent changes in working conditions,
increasing the power of labor and making purely servile toil
more or less obsolete, the spread of education to the masses and
generally the impact of new modes of communication, the competition of the great powers to win over to their respective sides the
new have-not peoples, and so forth. But we are dealing with a
secular process of universal range, and we might look for deeper
roots for a growth so sturdy and persistent. All forms of the
bondage of man to man rest on compulsion, direct physical compulsion where men are slaves or serfs, economic compulsion
where men's livelihood is wholly at the mercy of privileged property. Nearly always it generates deep-seated resentment, yearnings
for freedom, justice, retribution, that wait until the vicissitudes of
change provide opportunity for expansion. Occasions at length
arise when some members of the more privileged class take the
side of the subject group, whether because of ethical persuasions
or because they see an advantage for themselves in leading a
promising movement. Once such a movement takes hold it is
exceedingly difficult to suppress. It rallies behind it forces that
previously had been inert or indifferent. When, for example, the
urge for independence seizes a people, it is armed with a passion
that refuses to yield to much stronger opponents and costs the
other side so much that sooner or later they are likely to yield to
the demand for independence.

Power and the Sense of Inferiority (pages 193–196)

The role played by the sense of inferiority—or the fear of being treated as inferior—in the quest for power constitutes an illuminating chapter in the psychology of power. The relation of aggressiveness to the sense of inferiority has often been examined, as exhibited, for example, in the attitude of some members of minority groups or disprivileged groups. Aggressiveness may be developed not as a defense against an internal sense of inferiority but as a protest against the assumption of superiority on the part of those who occupy superior positions or who possess social privileges.

There are, however, various other ways than the aggressive approach in which a feeling of inferiority spurs the desire for power or for the facade of power. The victim of the feeling cherishes the thought that by "making good" he will overcome it. The expectation is most likely to be delusive—he feels as insecure in his new status as he did before. The sense of inadequacy or the uneasy need to assert his adequacy has infected his nerves and bitten into his mentality. He vainly seeks liberation by feeding his appetite for power.

Some of the characteristics that are frequently associated with the possession of power may themselves stem from a variety of the inferiority complex. The man of power tends to be aloof, and lonely. He must assert his difference from lesser men, the superiority of his judgment. So he cannot brook being contradicted, he dislikes critical advice. He demands obsequiousness in those who serve him. His pride is easily hurt. He must save face, no matter what it costs. Such not uncommon characteristics may be ex-

plicable as symptoms of the inner insecurity that the detachment
of the powerful from the common give-and-take of living is liable
to breed.

In our competitive unstable society, when position, status,
office are there for the winning and the losing, where there are
always higher niches to climb onto with precarious hold, where
fickle popularity bestows and withdraws success, where the young
are set standards to strive up to with little regard for their inclina-
tions or their capacities, the prevalence of inferiority feelings and
the struggle to evade or overcome them appear to be particularly
high. In simple societies and in class-bound societies everyone has
his assigned place, his lot in life. Status and power are predeter-
mined, and it is vain to kick against the pricks.

Index

235